40TH ANNIVERSARY EDITION

Styles for the Studio

A Foundation for Modern Guitar Improvisiation

LEON WHITE

© 1976 - 2016 Leon R. White · All Rights Reserved · StylesForTheStudio.com · info@stylesforthestudio.com

Version 3.0

Acknowledgments

DEDICATED TO JUDY WHITE

1976 Acknowledgments

I would like to take this time to thank those friends and associates whose assistance helped make this book possible:

Proof Reading (General Layout and Thought Content): Judy White

Proof Reading (Grammar and Verbal Usage): Jennie Gillespie

Photography: David Kessler and Associates

Cover Guitar: 1976 Fender Stratocaster from Mike McGuire and Al Carness at Valley Arts Guitar Center, Studio City, California

Typeset: Bob Campbell All proof copies by Len Mosk and Copymat, North Hollywood, California

For giving me the incentive to approach this subject in a book, I'd like to thank Judy White, Walter White, Jeffrey Brown, and all the fine musicians and teachers I've met, who could never explain the subject of improvising to me, to my own satisfaction.

At various points of completion, Ted Greene reviewed the total effort, giving generously of his wisdom, friendship, and emotional support as only he can - Thank You.

While many musicians have been influential to my playing, I'd like to thank the following for their efforts in this area: Judy White, Mike Warren, Jay Graydon, Dean Parks, and all those whose music I've come to know through my friendship with Ted Greene.

2016 Acknowledgments

A long list of people have kept contacting me over the years about 'Styles' and always with something kind to say. Gradually as the book became unavailable around 2011, there were requests to get copies as it was out of print in that year. The requests increased, and through the gracious folks at Alfred Publishing, I regained the copyright.

So to all who asked, I give you my deepest thanks. I hadn't opened the book in nearly 20 years, and when I did, I still liked it. When I started looking around, I understood why you might like it, and how it might help. On the advice of close friends I decided to re-release the book. For all the assistance with the mechanics of taking a paper copy back to digital form and publishing in this new environment, my biggest thank you is to Jeffrey Brown. It wouldn't have happened without all his hard work. And of course my sweetheart Judy is still the one that inspires me.

— *Leon White*

Cover Guitar: *Artist* model semi hollow-body courtesy of Sunset Guitars (mahogany body and spruce top)

Table of Contents

Acknowledgements	
Preface	
Introduction to the Student	1
Lesson 1 - Part A Improvising and the Language of Music	5
Lesson 1 - Part B Flat Pick Techniques	7
Lesson 2 - Fingering Notation	9
Lesson 3 - The Scale Fingering System	11
Lesson 4 - Major Scale Fingerings - Group One	12
Lesson 5 - Melodic Patterns	14
Lesson 6 - More Power - Connecting Positions Together	16
Lesson 7 - Applying Your Resources - The Major Scale	18
Lesson 8 - Examples of Melodies	19
Lesson 9 - String Bends	21
Lesson 10 - Preparing for Arpeggios - Chords and Degrees	23
Lesson 11 - The Arpeggio	24
Lesson 12 - Arpeggio Group #1 - G Major Scale 2e Fingering	25
Lesson 13 - Arpeggio Group #2 - A Major Scale 4e Fingering	27
Lesson 14 - Arpeggio Group #3 - F Major Scale 4a Fingering	29
Lesson 15 - Arpeggio Group #4 - C Major Scale 2a Fingering	30
Lesson 16 - Arpeggio Group #5 - G major Scale 1d Fingering	31
Lesson 17 - Arpeggio Group #6 - F Major Scale 1a Fingering	32
Lesson 18 - Arpeggio Group #7 - F Major Scale 1e Fingering	33
Lesson 19 - Part A - Arpeggio Review by Scale Fingering	34
Lesson 19 - Part B - Arpeggio Review by Fingering Shape	35
Lesson 20 - Arpeggio Review - Usage	37
Lesson 21 - Arpeggios and their Diatonic Extensions	38
Lesson 22 - The Diminished Seventh Arpeggio	40
Lesson 23 - A Word on Ear Training	42
Lesson 24 - New Scales	43
Lesson 25 - The Minor Pentatonic Scale	45
Lesson 26 - The Major Pentatonic Scale	47
Lesson 27 - The Dorian Scale	49
Lesson 29 - The Blues Scale	52
Lesson 29 - The Mixolydian Scale	54
Lesson 30 - Review Part A	56
Lesson 31 - Technique - Level Two	59
Lesson 32 - Part A - String Bends in Detail and by Position	61
Lesson 32 - Part B - String Bends and Their Relationship to Chords	63
Lesson 33 - Harmonized Scales	64
Lesson 34 - The Major Scale in Thirds	66
Lesson 35 - The Major Scale in Fourths and Sixths	69
Lesson 36 - Harmonizing Scales Other Than the Diatonic Major Scale	73
Lesson 37 - The Dorian Scale in Thirds and Sixths; The Mixolydian Scale in Thirds and Sixths	74
Lesson 38 - Bending Strings in Harmonized Scale Patterns	78
Lesson 39 - Bending Two Strings at Once	82
Harmony Quick Reference	85
Epilogue	88

Styles for the Studio by Leon White

Preface

This book was first written in 1976 (when there was still a studio business to be in). Although there is no longer a large and thriving studio player environment, the demands for those capabilities remain. The merging of musical styles and genres has country-style players adding fusion and cross-over sounds to their music. Jazz players routinely using nylon string guitars, and rock players turning up everywhere playing everything. The booming archtop guitar market (which didn't exist in 1976) is also proof of the merging and growth.

For this 40th Anniversary Edition we've

- maintained the original content,
- enlarged diagrams,
- removed some repetitive text,
- updated a few sections, and
- re-typeset the entire book.

Content has also been expanded in various parts. The only section to shrink is the reference on harmony, which has been reduced to only the material needed for *this* book. A larger discussion will be available separately.

The core of this book is to show you how music works on your guitar for improvising - the logic and the organization of tones that still govern a good melody and a good solo. The goal is still to end the confusion and uneasiness so many players feel when they don't know 'why' things work or how all the scales and fingerings fit together. The answer is in here. More importantly, the tools for you to make your own answers are in here too.

Note

There is a package of 100+ backing tracks, some additional notes, and a handful of videos available directly from Six String Logic at StylesfortheStudio.com. It is a single electronic bundle you can purchase and download. These are not jam tracks, but multiple versions of each chord progression example in the book at varying tempos and in varying styles. The bundle is a companion piece for the book.

Introduction to the Student

At some point every guitarist wants to be able to play a great guitar solo - not just a lick or fill - but a full-fledged solo that is fun to play, wows an audience, and makes the player feel good. We want to be able to play fluidly, play without technique limitations, get a great sound, and enhance the song. Behind that result is the ability to play what you feel whenever you want, and communicate something that moves your listeners.

To get there we need to learn to be great improvisers. This book discusses two of the two main areas of study that can fuel your success:

1. Understanding harmonic and melodic resources (scales, intervals, arpeggios, and fingerings); and
2. Learning how to apply those resources (technique and song knowledge).

"Understanding Harmonic resources" is the grand name for the chords, scales, arpeggios and harmony that can help when improvising.

"Applying the resources" includes understanding chord progressions, right hand and left hand techniques, and knowing which intervals in a scale convey which feelings.

Our goal is to help you to improvise and enjoy it; to show you where the various sounds are located, and how to apply them.

What Do You Need To Know to Get Started?

You should be able to do the following before starting this book:

1. Play the common barre chords.
2. Have a desire to "play lead."
3. Be aware of contemporary rock, blues, jazz, and/or country styles of music.
4. Have a guitar which you can play up to the twelfth fret.
5. Be studying, or already use, a flat pick. (This is not mandatory, but certain sounds depend upon a pick.)
6. Be at least starting to play with alternate picking ("Down-up down-up").

If you haven't thought about how you hold your guitar, you should do so. It is always advantageous to have your guitar in the same place in relation to your body and arms, whether you're standing or sitting. Consider using a strap in both positions to help you develop speed and control.

Your left hand should be free and comfortable in all of its movements along the neck. For this reason it is recommended that you strive for a hand posture that is slightly arched, loose and lets you play with the tips of your fingers.

There are several areas of music study that you should be aware of as you begin to use this book.

Below is a list of the musical topics a guitarist should be learning about at this stage.

1. You should be able to spell the major scales.
2. You should be able to spell the major and minor chords.
3. You should know what is meant by a "diatonic extension."
4. You should know what the word "chromatic" means.
5. You should know on which "degrees" of the scale the major and minor chords occur.
6. You should be familiar with the Roman numeral system of naming chords.

It is important to learn at least a little harmony and theory. That knowledge can answer a lot of questions you'll have, and also *accelerate* your progress in improvising. It simplifies a lot of other information, and is a super shortcut for everything you can learn on the guitar. This book is about learning quickly - keep on the lookout for things that help you learn the fastest - be self-aware!

What Are We Going To Be Working On?

1. We're going to establish a framework for all scale and arpeggio fingerings. (They are *not* random, so let's exploit their organization.)
2. We're going to learn to recognize certain sounds in melodies, and where to find them.
3. We're going to work through each fingering for each scale to find the sounds we want.
4. We're going to compare and 'overlay' the fingerings from different scales to see how they fit together.
5. We will explore the arpeggio fingerings found *inside* the major scale fingerings.
6. We'll explore right hand and left hand techniques for making music out of the sounds we're learning.
7. We'll use sample melodies and chord progressions to tie the sounds to chord progressions.
8. We'll have some fun and feel like something was accomplished (I hope).

A Brief Outline of this Book

Topics covered include (1) The Diatonic Major Scale, and its arpeggios, and (2) "Rock" scales, including the Minor Pentatonic, Major Pentatonic, Dorian, Mixolydian and Blues scale.

Part One - The Major Scale - Fundamentals, Fingerings, Arpeggios, and Technique

- Fundamentals (How the diagrams work, fingering names, and general housekeeping for getting started)
- The Major Scale - Fingerings and applications (*emphasizing small intervals*)
- The sounds of the root, 2, 3, 4, 5, 6, and ♮7 notes)
- The Melodic pattern - A tool for making melodies from scales
- Techniques like string bends (up and down); bending in tune, and more

Part Two - The Arpeggios in the Major scale - Fingerings and Examples

- Diatonic arpeggios of 4 note chords in the Major scale - Maj7, Min7, Dominant 7, Min7♭5 sounds (*emphasizing large intervals*)
- Arpeggios with diatonic extensions (9ths, 13ths, 6/9s etc.)

Part Three – New Scales and Techniques for Rock, Blues, and Country

- The Minor Pentatonic Scale (adding the ♭3 and ♭7 notes to what we know)
- The Major Pentatonic Scale (emphasizing the 6th and 9th sounds)
- The Blues Scale (introducing the ♯4 note using a minor pentatonic set of sounds)
- The Dorian Scale (showing us the ♭3 and ♭7 sounds together like the minor pentatonic, but adding the 6th and 9th notes too)
- The Mixolydian Scale (focusing our ears on the combination of ♮3 and ♭7 together)
- Techniques discussion - Tips on string bending and other effects

Part Four - Playing Two Notes at a Time: "Double Stops" and Harmonized Scales

- The Diatonic Major Scale Harmonized – Fingerings in different intervals (thirds, fourths, sixths)
- Harmonizing the Dorian and Mixolydian Scales
- Bending Strings inside Harmonized Scales (bending one of two strings being played)
- Bending *both* strings (and notes) at the same time ("Ow!")

Reference - Selected Notes on Basic Harmony

Options for Using This Book

There are two ways in which you may study this book:
- You can study on your own
- You can study with a teacher, as many teachers have written to tell me. (Thanks to all of you!)

In terms of the content, there are several ways to work through the book. The outline, again, is:

1. Getting started stuff (diagrams, numbering fingers, scale names etc.)
2. Major scales and introductory techniques like string bends
3. Major scale arpeggios
4. Rock, Country and Blues scales
5. Rock techniques including pedal tones, bends, double bends, etc.

Some players may want to jump to section four for the various scale sounds. However, underneath all the scales, arpeggios, and samples is a *single organization* of fingerings and sounds. They all fit together to cover the entire neck in any key.

Knowing at least the *outline* of that organization (shown in part two) will make the *whole book* go much faster. It can also answer a lot of questions you may have as you improvise more.

Even if you don't memorize all seven major scale fingerings, you should at least understand how they are setup and interlock with each other. The whole point of the fingering model is to get you to the point where you will be able to *forget* fingerings when soloing. Seeing and *hearing* this organization in the major scale will get you there faster.

Teachers: The Fingering Madness Revealed

Major Scale	Blues Scale
Arpeggios	Dorian Scale
Minor Pentatonic Scale	Major Pentatonic Scale
Mixolydian Scale	

Wow, that is a lot of scales and fingerings!?! I'm going to come clean here for the first time in print: There are really 7 physical fingering positions and shapes for all of this. Here's what I mean:

The major scale really has seven basic shapes. Those fingerings also cover the Dorian, Mixolydian, and Major Pentatonic fingerings out of the box.

The diatonic arpeggios are also part of each major scale fingering, as each contains only selected notes from a fingering you'll already know. (And even those arpeggio fingerings overlap with each other!) So the major scale fingerings cover these arpeggios.

The Minor Pentatonic scale is only one note away from a minor seventh arpeggio (you just add the 4th, or "11th" to the sound). The Blues Scale is a minor pentatonic with a raised 4th degree added (#4 or #11th or even called a ♭5th). The rest of the notes are the same! Again we have shapes like those found in the arpeggios and major scales. Really.

When you're comfortable with the 7 fundamental major scale fingerings (physically that is) you've seen about all the physical challenges you can see. The rest of the work is in hearing and making melodies - finding the notes you want when you want them. Everything is transposable, so we shouldn't worry about that. What you do have to do is learn to *hear the notes and intervals* internally and find them on the guitar fluidly. That is what we'll do.

Diagrams Used in this Book

The following Diagrams are used throughout this book to illustrate fingerings on the guitar fretboard for scales, arpeggios, string bends, and sample melodies.

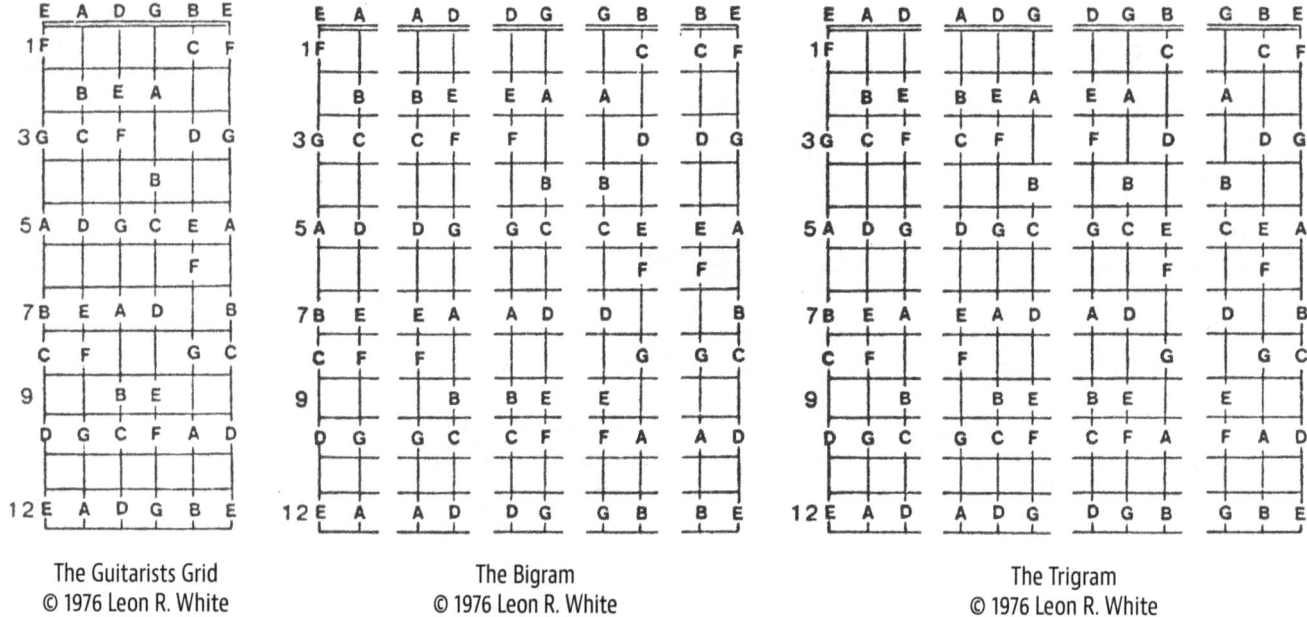

The Guitarists Grid
© 1976 Leon R. White

The Bigram
© 1976 Leon R. White

The Trigram
© 1976 Leon R. White

The **Guitarists Grid** shows the six strings of the guitar. The locations of the "natural notes" are included as guides to where you are. ("natural notes" because they have no sharps or flats: C, D, E, F, G, A, and B)

The **Bigram** divides the six strings of the guitar into PAIRS of adjacent strings. Note that the fifth string (the A) appears twice in the Bigram - once in each pair of strings it is in. Take your guitar and grab two strings (next to each other). Now repeat this with other pairs. That is what the Bigram does.

The **Trigram** does exactly the same thing, but uses groups of *three* adjacent strings. Grab three strings (next to each other) and you'll see how the Trigram works.

We are going to locate notes on these diagrams by circling them. This will indicate you are to play the circled notes.

On occasion a circle will have NO LETTER NAME inside it. This means that we want you to play a note that is between one of the seven "natural" notes which are shown on the diagrams. This note is not less important. It's just like the other notes, except its name is not on the diagram forms we're using. Showing only the natural notes keeps the diagrams less cluttered and easier to read.

Lesson 1 · Part A

Improvising and the Language of Music

Music has often been called a "language." How do you learn to speak? You are exposed to words of the language gradually, usually starting with only one or two, like "Mama," "Papa," or ... "Guitar" (?) Once you know a few words (that is, a basic vocabulary) your learning pattern changes. New words are defined and explained in terms of "old" words whose meanings are already clear to you. It is a building process. The better you understand the beginning "foundation" words, the more quickly and easily you will be able to understand new words.

The "words" of music are our musical tones and intervals. We're going to start with some you know, and use those to build out your improvising sounds.

Definitions

INTERVAL: The distance between any TWO notes. Intervals only exist if you have at least two notes. The word interval also refers to the sound of going from one note to the next. Different distances between notes (i.e. different intervals) affect human beings differently. Some intervals are "happy," some are sad or morose, and so on. We will examine this in more detail as we proceed. You can make up your own mind about these as you experiment and investigate. For now all you need to know is that (1) There are different intervals and (2) They each affect us differently. Play the notes in the diagram one note at a time as numbered (#1 then #2).

Now play the notes of the diagram *together*.

Melodic Intervals: The interval between two notes played in succession — that is, one after the other.

Harmonic Intervals: Interval sounds created when two notes are played *together*. "Melodic" refers to "in a melody", while "Harmonic" refers to notes played together, as in a chord. *Can you hear that two notes played one after the other can have a vastly different "feeling" from the same two notes played together?*

Scale: A succession of pitches in a fixed order. There may be any number of notes, in any order. Scales put notes in groups from which all our music may be built. Chords are made from scales, and solos (and melodies) are made from notes in scales.

Accidental: The name of the symbols that can be part of a note name. The sharp #, the flat ♭, and the natural ♮ are all "accidentals."

Diatonic Major Scale: The scale that fixes notes in the following sequence of half step and whole step intervals.

Degree (or "Scale Degree"): The notes in a scale can be given numbers when listed alphabetically. In the scale above C is the "first degree," E is the "third degree."

Roman Numerals in Scales: One popular way of discussing chords found in a scale is to name the chord after its degree. When doing so, Roman numerals can be used when writing it. The "two chord" could be written like this: ii chord. The "five chord" could be written as "V chord." We'll see more on this in just a few pages.

Scales are a powerful device for improvising and a very good way to become familiar with interval sounds. We will study the Diatonic Major scale first as it is the most familiar to your ear. After we are familiar with this scale (the "granddaddy" of our western music) we'll learn other scales that are popular in today's country-rock-jazz-music, including the following:

1. The Minor Pentatonic Scale
2. The Major Pentatonic Scale
3. The Dorian Scale
4. The Mixolydian Scale
5. The Blues Scale

(Although each of these scales has its own sound, you'll probably recognize all these sounds as we progress.)

One Scale Per Chord or One Scale Per Progression?

Another important feature of ALL of these scales is their simplicity of use. We are using them over a whole progression of chords.

For instance: In a blues progression in the Key of C you might use
1. A "C" Blues scale,
2. A "C" Dorian scale, or
3. One of the "C" Pentatonic scales.

Which one you use depends on *your* taste regarding the sounds; all could 'work' over the entire progression.
- All of the fingerings of *all* the scales are based on one system, which overlaps and interlocks. You will not be learning hundreds of fingerings - only a few.
- All of the fingerings and fingering *names* are based around the ROOT of the scale (often the key). That is - in our C Blues example above, you'll know just where to go to get a C Dorian scale. There will be no confusion.
- All the scale fingerings can be moved up and down the fingerboard to other keys. So once you learn the fingerings for a C Mixolydian scale (for example) you'll know the Mixolydian fingerings for the keys of A, D, F#, B, E, etc.

Scales and Modes

In traditional explanations of harmony study the term "scale" is treated as a more important concept then the term "mode." Why? Because, by definition, a "mode" is a group of notes *derived* from a scale. Originally there was the "Major Scale" and "modes" were created by playing the major scale from a note other than the root. For example:

C Major Scale	C D E F G A B C
D Dorian *Mode*	D E F G A B C D ("D to D")
G Mixolydian *Mode*	G A B C D E F G ("G to G")

While both true and interesting, in modern improvising this distinction can confuse players in a number of ways. "When you see a G7 chord, just play a C major scale from the G note." Say what?

I prefer to simplify improvisation by thinking about the sounds, and NOT their historical sources. So, in this book I'll treat modes and scales as scales, and refer to them as scales. Those of you that love modes - don't get mad at me! I like modes as much as the next music major (UCLA for me). In improvisation (and even modern composing) the functional use of both can be the same, so we'll treat them as the same.

When you progress to improvising over songs with chords from different keys mushed together, thinking from the root of the chord will be easier, simpler, and faster. More importantly, we're trying to *train your ear* to recognize intervals (big or small) from a standard point - the root. This approach will help you there as well.

Try this approach on for size before you make up your mind. It makes improvising a LOT easier, and eliminates most of the "harmonic minor with a natural 6th note played from the 5th of the scale" kind of craziness. I mean no disrespect to those that teach with another approach, but for me it assumes you'll "think" all the time when improvising. The ideal solo comes straight from the heart. It doesn't always have time to stop off at the brain. Sadly, we're not always ready to let go and play, but we can try.

Lesson 1 - Part B

Flat Pick Techniques

"Alternate picking" is being able to play an up stroke or a down stroke with even, firm control. The key is to get a good sound from either direction. The following exercises will help cure deficiencies in several problem areas that occur in alternate picking. Start to include these in your practice or warm-ups now.

Exercise A - On One String

Try alternating up and down strokes on one string only. Each note should be clean, clear, and of equal volume. Play slowly and evenly. This is a simple exercise, but it is *very* important. Your goal should be to speed up or slow down your picking speed smoothly, and with full control. Like scale fingerings, this effort is designed to get you to a point where you forget about it and just play.

Exercise B - On Two Strings

Play alternate strokes on two strings at a time; once again begin slowly. Strive for equal volume and control.

Exercise C - On Three, Four, Five, and Six Strings

Repeat the above exercise on 3, 4, 5 and 6 strings, respectively. Can you hear the difference between a smooth, steady up and down stroke on four strings and on five? On six? Here is a good opportunity to practice any chords you are learning.

Try and get a smooth even 'rolling' sound. Increase the speed of your up and down strokes gradually, until you can really control a fast 'roll.' (This is the sound you hear in live concerts at the end of a song when the band just stays on one chord. They're all playing and the leader takes his guitar and waves it in a big motion to end the song, like trying to flag down a train.)

"String Crossing"

Being able to play single notes on different strings with alternating strokes is very important. If you stumble or stop all together when you try to play a fast scale, run, or "lick," exercises 1 and 2 should help.

Exercises 3 and 4 will help cure the problem of alternate picking on strings NOT adjacent to each other. Take your time here. There are some surprising sounds on non-adjacent strings.

Exercise One

Play this exercise using alternate picking continuously. Play the notes in this order: G D A, C G D, F C G, and B♭ F C. To play "Back", play the notes in this order: B♭ F C, F C G, C G D, G D A. (Don't reverse the notes in each group of three, just move the three notes to a new string set.) Hold down your fingers on each set of three strings. This is very important. If this reach is too large for your hand, move it up the neck until it feels more comfortable.

#1

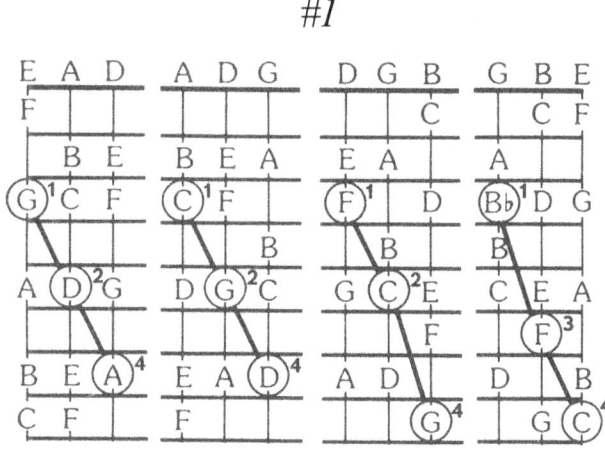

The first technique examples I learned came from Mike Warren. "Alternate picking on alternate strings in triplets." For more right hand control, hold down each set of three notes and play those three strings together. Use alternate picking and play the set of strings down-up four times.

Exercise Two

Play the notes in this exercise in the order they are numbered in diagram A. Use the fingers shown on the right. Once you've played this 6-note pattern on one fret, move it up one fret and repeat it. Continue all the way up the fingerboard. To return down the fingerboard, play the notes in the order shown in diagram B.
Use the fingers indicated at the right. Play the 6-note pattern on one fret, and then move it up one fret and repeat it. Continue moving it up until you have reached the top of your guitar. This exercise should also be played on the other strings on your guitar.

Exercise Three

Play the notes in Exercise 3 with alternate strokes (down up, down up). Start with a down stroke on the G note. Play the notes in this order: G G A# F#. Then move over one string and play the same pattern. (Here it will be C C E♭ B). Continue across the fingerboard in this way.

To "play across the fingerboard" with all of these patterns, you just move to another pair of strings. This is important to remember when you try to play back (that is, from the treble strings to the bass strings). Do NOT reverse the order in which you play the notes! Simply repeat the pattern as you have been playing it, but move back to a new pair of strings.

Exercise Four

This is similar to Exercise 3 except that the notes are in a different sequence. Play them in this order: G# G#, A F. Use alternate picking. As before, move this exercise across the strings.

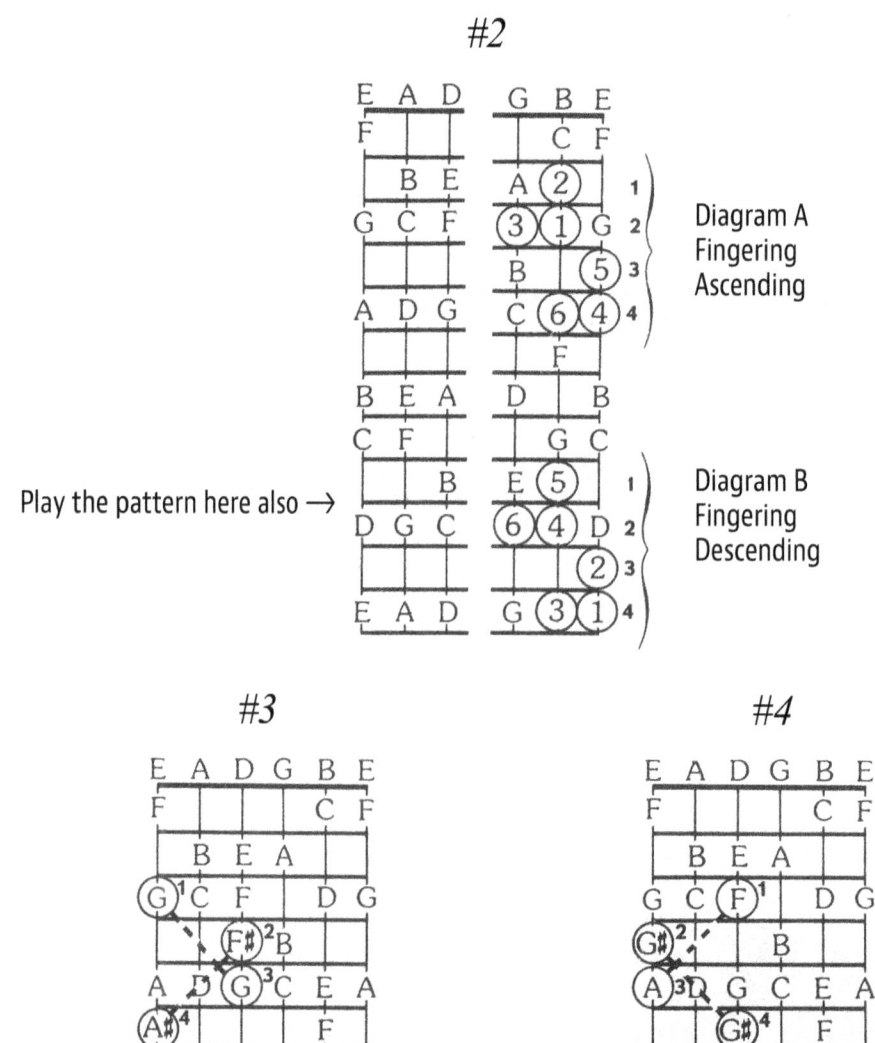

Styles for the Studio by Leon White • 8

Lesson 2

Fingering Notation

We are going to begin by learning fingerings for the major scale. Don't skip anything, because we are laying the groundwork here for everything else that is to follow.

Our System of Notation

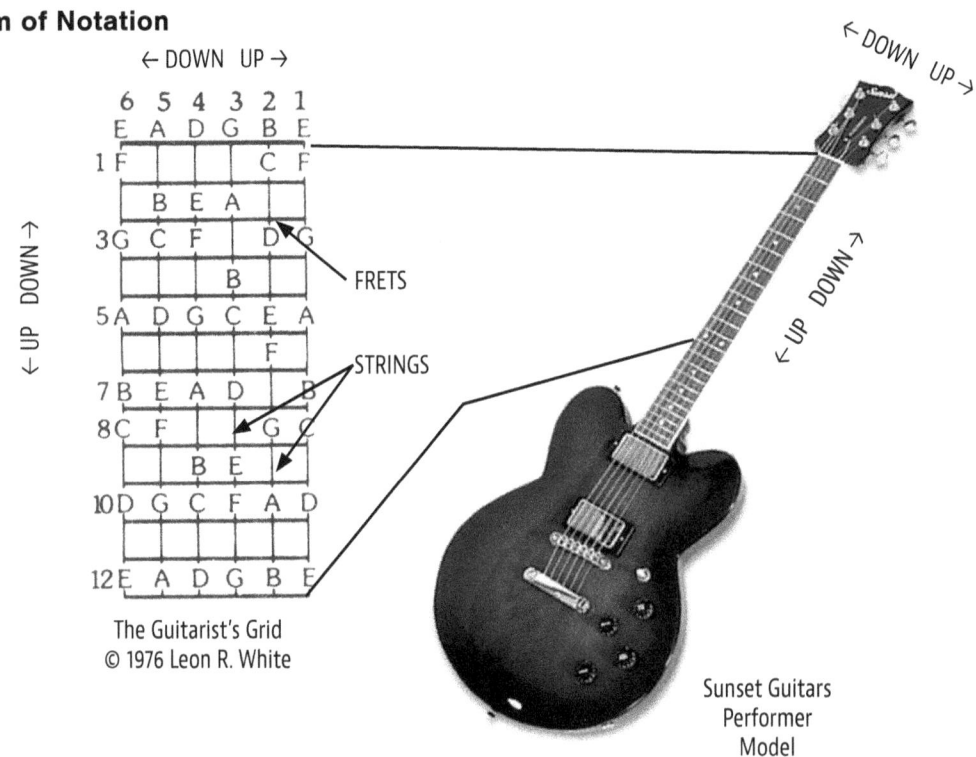

The Guitarist's Grid
© 1976 Leon R. White

Sunset Guitars
Performer
Model

Above is a picture showing how the Guitarists Grid© relates to the fingerboard of the guitar. There are the six strings shown, with the location of the "natural" notes shown on each string.

On the Guitarists Grid© we will circle each note you are to play for any particular fingering. A Square (□) shows the root of the fingering - the starting point in playing it. Optional notes that are available in the fingering location will be shown with a dotted circle (⊙). These notes may appear above or below the root of the fingering, however, the most important note is that root - our *point of reference visually and sonically*.

"Below ... Above ... Ascending ... Descending ... Up ... Down ..." What do we mean when we use these words to describe motion on the fingerboard, or in music?

We will use these words to describe movement in musical *pitch*.

In the following diagram, the G note is "higher" than the E note.

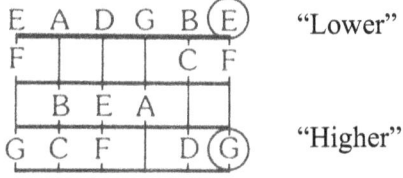

"Lower"

"Higher"

Playing "up the neck," or "up a scale,"
means playing up *in pitch*. In the example above, if you played the E note first, and then the G note, you would be playing "up." or "ascending." "Down" and "descending" mean just the opposite of "up."

Since you can change strings as you play a scale or melody, UP can also mean across the fingerboard (left to right in the next diagram). The notes are numbered in *ascending* order in that diagram. The right-hand diagram below shows the same notes numbered in *descending* order.

Which fingers play which notes in scales and arpeggios?"

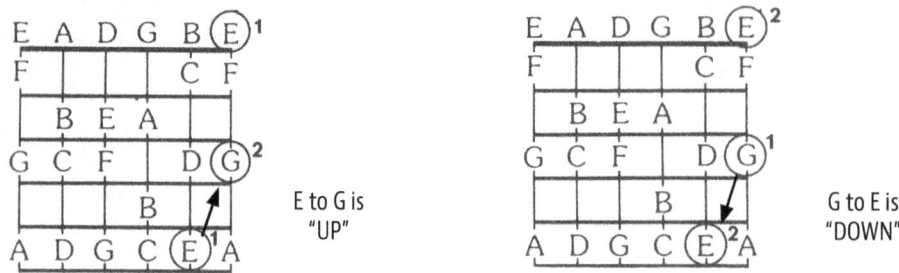

E to G is "UP"

G to E is "DOWN"

1. Our basic rule is - ONE FINGER PER FRET (Diagram #1 below)

2. The 1st and 4th FINGERS MAY STRETCH, one fret each, from the original position (Diagram #2).

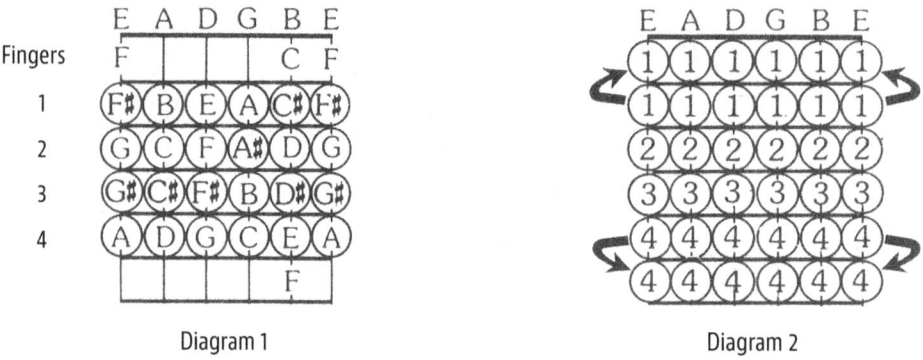

Diagram 1

Diagram 2

3. The same finger occupies the same fret on all strings, in any single fingering position. (Diagram #3, below).
4. Once you've learned a fingering, all you have to do is the find the *root* to start. You should then be able to *feel* the rest of the notes (and sounds) from there.

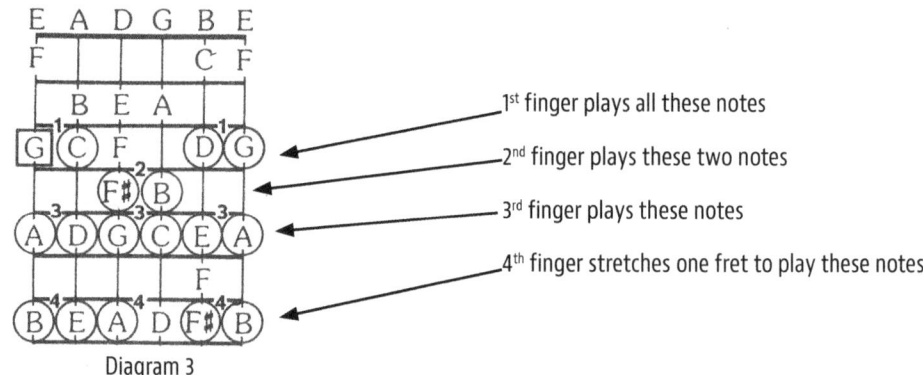

1st finger plays all these notes
2nd finger plays these two notes
3rd finger plays these notes
4th finger stretches one fret to play these notes

Diagram 3

Lesson 3

The Scale Fingering System

The fingerings for all scales and arpeggios are based on the single system shown here with the major scale. There are seven patterns that cover the entire neck.

(Since the original edition of this book, the "CAGED" scale fingering system has become popular – there are five fingerings, roughly, depending on who's teaching them.) Those five are included within our *seven* fingerings. CAGED is workable for rock and blues, but we really *do* need the extra two fingerings.

The seven fingerings give you everything you'll need. I hope you learn the fingerings once and get it out of the way. It is important to note that these fingerings are also used to read music, and handle the "outside" sounds in improvisation.

Chords and arpeggios will also fall into these *same seven* fingerings. For example:

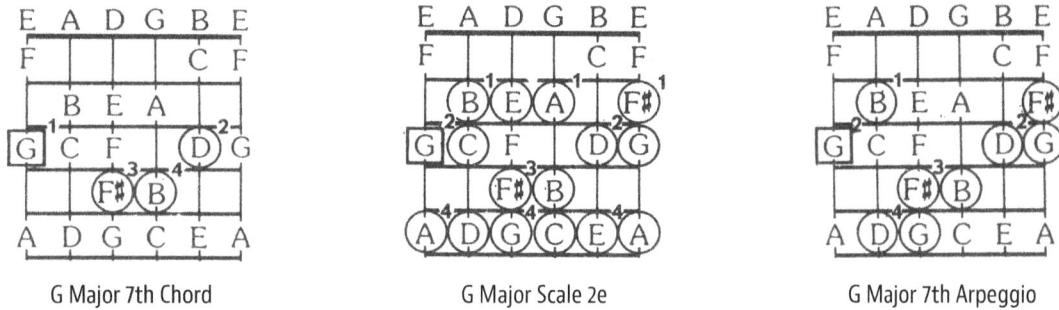

G Major 7th Chord   G Major Scale 2e   G Major 7th Arpeggio

Everything you'll see is based on this same system, so it will be easy to remember. It will re-inforce the *sounds* you're learning and their locations. This interlocking system of patterns could only occur with an organization based on SOUND. (There are seven notes in a major scale, most modes, and altered dominant jazz scales. That is where the seven comes from. Can you see why?)

We'll start by memorizing a few of them to give you some context for your beginning improvising.

Fingering Names

The pattern names DESCRIBE the scale fingering; the name has two parts - the name of the root, and a number and letter for the fingering shape. The number stands for the left hand finger that begins the pattern FROM THE LOWEST ROOT, while the letter represents the name of the string that has the lowest root (our point of reference). For example:

The G scale "1e" pattern name means "a G major scale beginning with the 1st finger (playing the root - G) on the low E string" (see the diagram below). All the patterns are movable and may be played in other keys. Please note that these fingerings place equal emphasis on ALL FOUR of your left hand fingers. If you had a weak pinky when you bought this book, you probably won't when you finish it.

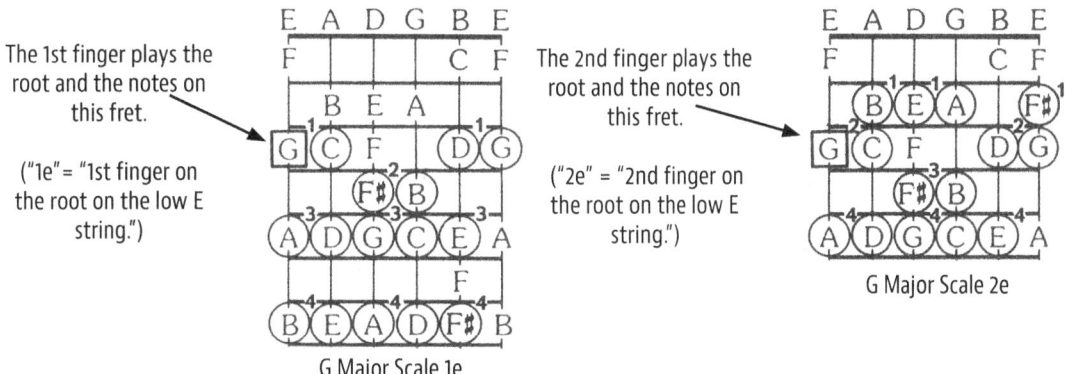

Styles for the Studio by Leon White • 11

Lesson 4

Major Scale Fingerings - Group One

Below are the first four major scale fingerings. The square indicates the root of the scale. Play the scale by starting on the lowest root, and playing up the scale to the highest note in the fingering.

The first fingering, G-2e is started with your second finger on the low G note. The second fingering, G-1e is started with your first finger on the low G note.

Shown next to each scale fingering are chords found within the fingering (for the first two fingerings they will be G chords).

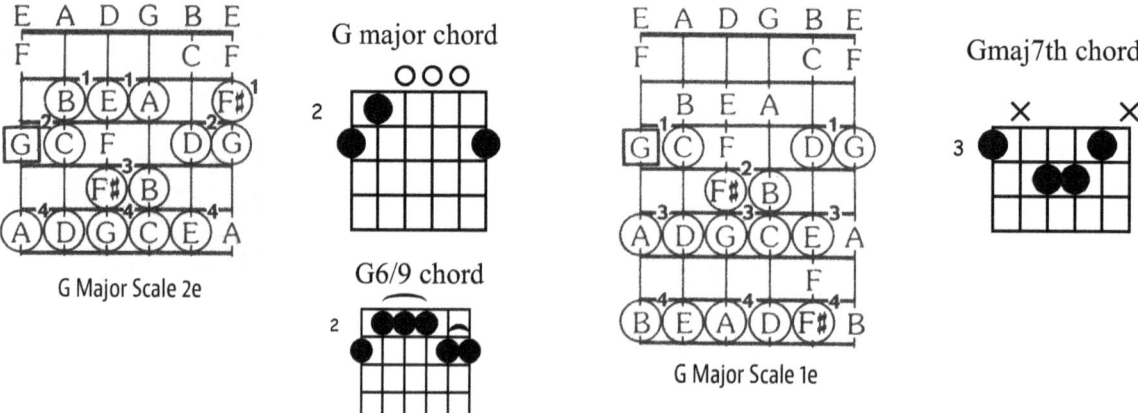

To learn each fingering, begin by playing slowly up the scale. Try to use alternate picking ("down-up-down-up").

At first you should work on the fingering by playing up the scale again and again. Do *NOT* play down the scale. Once you can play the scale ascending in a smooth and steady manner, start playing ascending, and then descending. Speed is *not* the objective here. The objective is to play the scale with a smooth and steady volume in a regular even speed. The sound of each note should be clean - no fret buzzes or out of tune notes (from pressing too hard).

Shown below are the third and fourth scale fingerings. The third fingering is shown from the root G located on the 4th string (the D string). Begin by playing this fingering ascending from the root G.

When you are comfortable enough to play it ascending and descending, start from the G note ascending, then play *all the way down to the A note on the lowest string*, and then back up to the root G on the 4th string. Make sure you keep the G major sound clearly in your head as you play by always *ending* on the root.

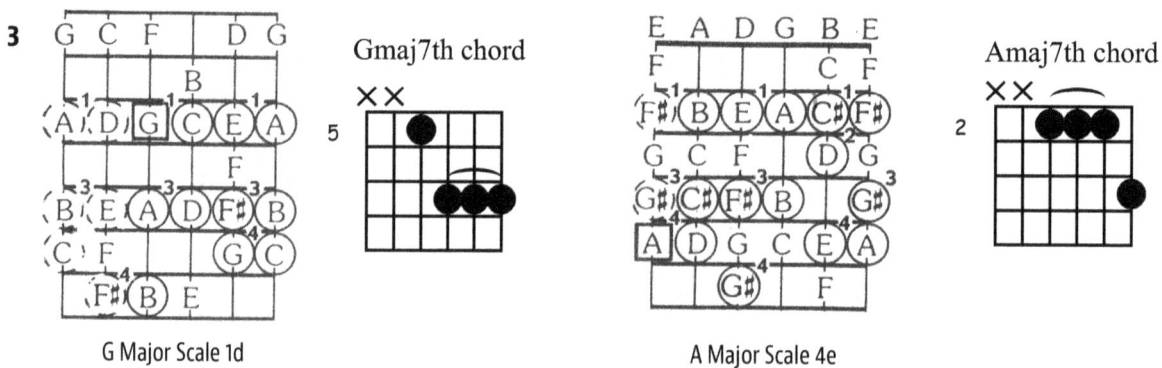

The fourth fingering, A-4e, is played from the root A starting on the 5th fret of the E string. Learn as before, and when you are able to play down below the root A, be sure to come back and end on the A. Again, this is to keep the A tonal center in mind as you practice this fingering.

Making Music with the Major Scales

Although we're just starting out, as you memorize the first few fingerings you should try to play melodies of some kind. This should be an experimental step only.

Starting on a note in the G fingerings like G, play up the scale in this way: G - G - A - B. Play at an even speed and play two G notes followed by the next note in the scale, A, and then the next note in the scale, B. (These are notes 1, 2, and 3 in all of the scale fingerings when playing from the root G.) Hold the B note so it sustains longer than the other notes.

For accompaniment, use a backing track of these chords:

```
G       G      Amin   D
////   ////   ////   ////
```

For example above, the slash line (/) represents 1 beat. You can play the chords in any strum pattern as long as each chord symbol receives 4 beats, and the tempo isn't fast. To begin your experiment, play the melody starting from the 1st beat; then play the melody from the first beat of each chord. Continue your experimenting by playing up *and then down* the three notes. From there you can try anything you want as long as you stay "in" the G major scale (that is, playing only the notes found inside the G major scale fingerings).

It is a small and simple start, but thinking about experimenting, and trying different ideas in a simple setting will help you create great solos, transcribe, and become comfortable with each fingering.

Major Scale Fingerings – Group Two

The fingerings in this group begin with the ROOT on the low A string (the 5th string). As before the 1a fingering requires some stretching, but as you'll see in a few pages, the 1a fingering is one of the most important.

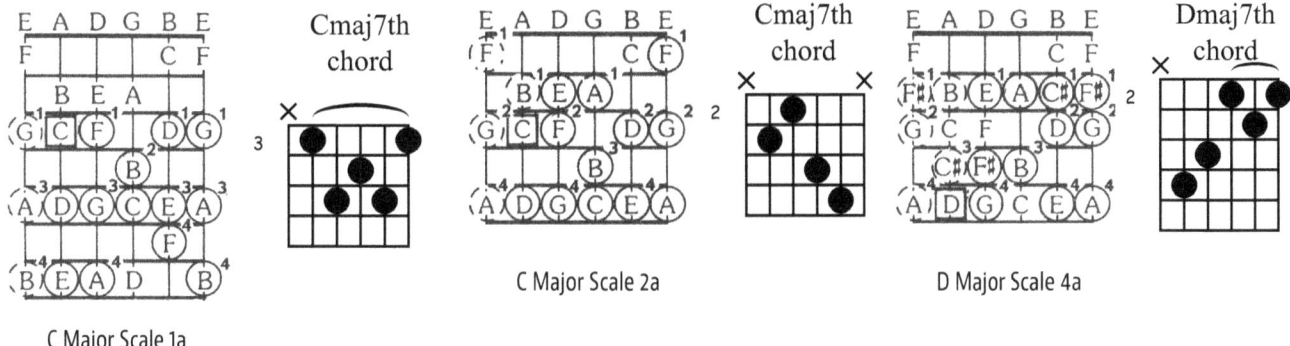

C Major Scale 1a   C Major Scale 2a   D Major Scale 4a

Some major scale fingerings, like C-1a above, can seem a little difficult at first because of the stretching you may feel. This will disappear if you keep playing. Some of the greatest blues and rock solos come out of these fingerings so don't ignore them.

Tips for learning a new fingering:

1. At first play only one octave of the fingering and then play it back to the root. Repeat this until you're confident with it. Then add the second octave (or higher part of the fingering) and repeat.
2. Play each new fingering slowly. Starting slowly will cut your learning time almost in half.
3. Use alternate picking. At first it may seem clumsy or difficult, but simply repeating it will solve the problem. If you're still having trouble after 10 minutes of scale playing, play more slowly.
4. Work on several fingerings at the same time. This helps keep you from becoming bored, and gives each left hand finger proper exercise. If your hand or fingers hurt, stop for a minute. No INJURIES!
5. Try to make little melodies in each fingering.
6. Listen for noises, squeaks, and buzzes, and try to work them out of the fingering. (As long as you're practicing *playing* you might as well practice listening). This is *very* important!

Lesson 5

Melodic Patterns

(By now you should be getting comfortable with several scale positions.) A melodic pattern is a short melody played from each note in the scale. They are your first "tools" for making music from scales. They will help you memorize your scales and also help you become fluent in playing them. (You'll also find that melodic patterns are excellent for building "riffs" too!)

1. Work with each melodic pattern in your most comfortable scale fingering first. You may have trouble playing them "back" but that is natural. (If you learn a pattern ascending, descending might trip you up initially.) If you need to, practice them only ascending at first, until you're confident with that. Then learn them descending.
2. The next task is to try the melodic pattern in a different fingering. The sound will help you find your way in the new fingerings.
3. With two fingerings comfortable under your fingers you can work on new material while taking the old pattern into a new fingering as a background task. All this effort does one important thing - it helps your brain learn where the sounds are located on the neck.
4. You'll use these patterns A LOT! The melodic patterns can be used with any scale (major, minor, ruhbarbian, or even delorean).

As it will be shown:

The notes are played in the order they are numbered beneath the staff.

Look at the notes as they appear on the Guitarist's Grid.

Remember: All of our Melodic Patterns will be shown in a shorthand notation.
1. We will show a portion of each melodic pattern.
2. We will use only the C major scale to demonstrate the pattern. Remember that the patterns can be played in any fingering in any key.

You should always use alternate picking (pick down on the first note, up on the second, down on the third, and so on). To help build up strength in your picking, you can also reverse that motion - pick UP on the first note, DOWN on the second, and so on as you practice. (That can really help your playing!)

Melodic patterns are a fabulous way to learn a fingering, learn to hear melodies in the scale, and improve your left hand finger dexterity (the pattern puts notes in different order, so on occasion, you'll have some new finger moves to learn). They also feed your brain with short patterns that turn themselves into licks with repetition.

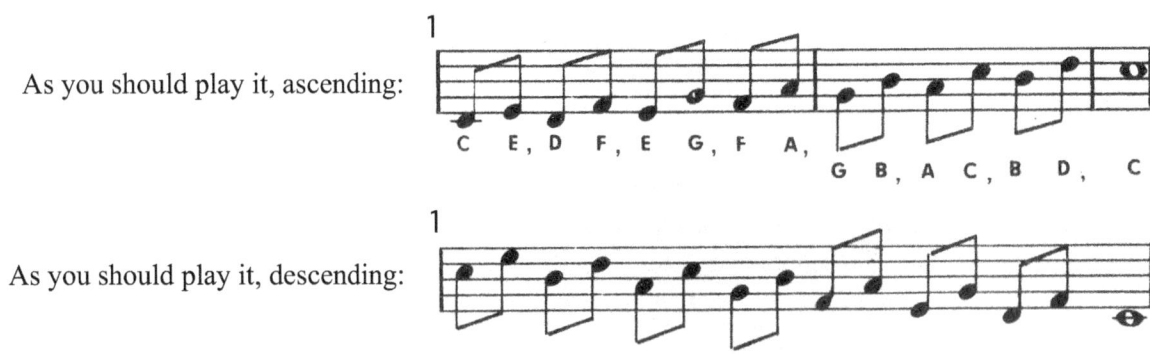

There are two fundamental rhythms you can use to play a melodic pattern as you begin:
- "one and, two and, three and, four and" - these notes are grouped in pairs (see ex. 2)
- "one-trip-let" - This is a three-note figure. In this rhythm the notes are grouped together in threes.
  Say "one trip-let." That's what a "triplet" sounds like. (See examples 3. 4, 5, and 7)

Here are the first four Melodic Patterns. Play these patterns from your scale fingerings, in this order - 2e, 4e, 1e, 2a, 4a, 1a, 1d.

- #2 (Shown ascending completely) - a four note pattern with the first note of each four being the scale tone and point of reference.
- #3 (Shown ascending completely) - once again the first note of each group of three is the scale tone.
- #4 Triplets of "thirds" - The first note is the point of reference in each pattern.
- #5 This is #4 with the second pattern played descending.
- #6 This is a pattern based on the interval of a fourth.   C D E F (C)   D E F G
-   1 2 3 4   1 2 3 4
- #7 This melodic pattern is really a "sequence." A sequence can be a short pattern based around the *tones of a chord*. In this example the chord is C Major 7th (C E G B).
- #8 A large interval pattern starting with a sixth.   C D E F G A
                                                          1 2 3 4 5 6

Alternate pick each of these patterns.

Lesson 6

More Power - Connecting Positions Together

As you improvise, you do not want to be limited to only one location on the guitar fingerboard. The primary reason for learning "positions" is to help you organize and visualize the fingerboard in small 'bites.' As you become familiar with these different "pieces" of the fingerboard puzzle, you will be able to fit them together to form a complete "picture" of the fingerboard. AND, you'll STOP seeing positions and just play.

Now that you are becoming familiar with the Major scale positions (you may not know them all yet), we'd like to show you how they connect together. To use the diagrams follow the steps below. We're working in the key of G major in this lesson.

Step 1. In Diagram 1, play from low G up to high A.

Step 2. Now, with your fourth finger on that high A note, slide up two frets, to the next note in the G Scale. (Key of G, right?) (Here slide from A up to B.)

Step 3. Congratulations, you are now in position 1e. Play down this scale fingering, and then back up, to this high B. (This is Diagram #2.)

Step 4. Now, with your fourth finger on B, slide it up to the next scale tone (here slide from B to C).

Step 5. (Diagram 3) Hooray! You are now in position 1d. Play down and then back up this fingering.

Step 6. Let's slide from that high C up to D.

Step 7. If your fourth finger is on high D, you are now in position 4a (Diagram 4). Play down and up here too.

Step 8. (Diagram 4) Slide the high D up to E. If you do this, you are now in scale position 2a. (See following page for diagrams)

Step 9. Play down and up this 2a scale position, and then from that E note slide up to F# you will be in a 1a scale position.

Step 10. Slide from F# to G. You're now in position 4e. Play up and down the scale in this position.

To finish, slide from the G up to A. You are now back where you started - position 2e, Key of G.

To move down, just reverse the process. For instance - Start in position 1d. Slide your FIRST finger from A, *down* to G. You just moved into position 1e.

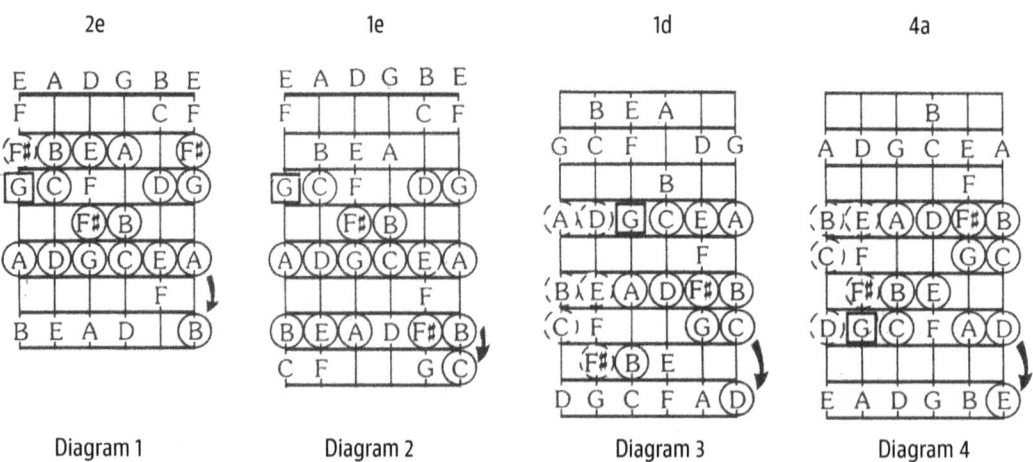

Diagram 1 Diagram 2 Diagram 3 Diagram 4

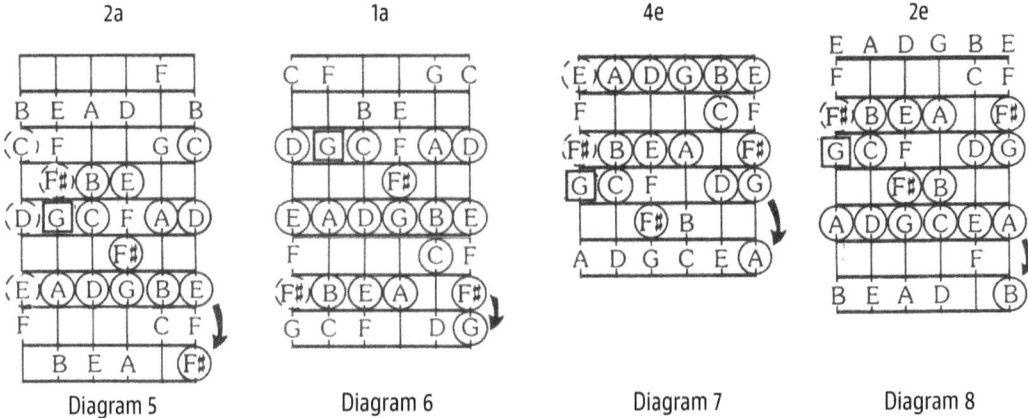

Diagram 5   Diagram 6   Diagram 7   Diagram 8

This same sequence of fingering positions will work for all of the scales in the first part of this book (Major, Dorian, and Mixolydian). The Pentatonic Scales fits in here as well, but in a slightly different way.

Practice shifting up and down from each position into the proper neighboring position. To do this start in any position and slide on the first string as we discussed above.

Moving "Down" in Pitch

If you were trying to move from position 1d, BACK to position 1e, move *down with your first finger.*

Think and move with your first finger when moving down, and with your fourth when moving up, whenever possible. Why? Because these two fingers occupy notes that are on the "outside" of the fingerings, and are therefore the simplest to track.

A more advanced idea ... You can move from "outside" notes, *on any string,* when shifting to a new position. Try it. Take the 1e position, and on the third or fourth strings slide up (with a note fingered with your fourth finger) to the next note in the scale.

The Entire Neck in the Key of G Major

Shown below are all seven scale fingerings, in relation to the neck to each other. These fingerings overlap and interlock to allow you to play anywhere on the board. The seven fingerings played in order, will move up the neck one scale note at a time. The order of the fingerings is G-2e, G-1e, G-1d, G-4a, G-2a, G-1a, G-4e, and G-2e again.

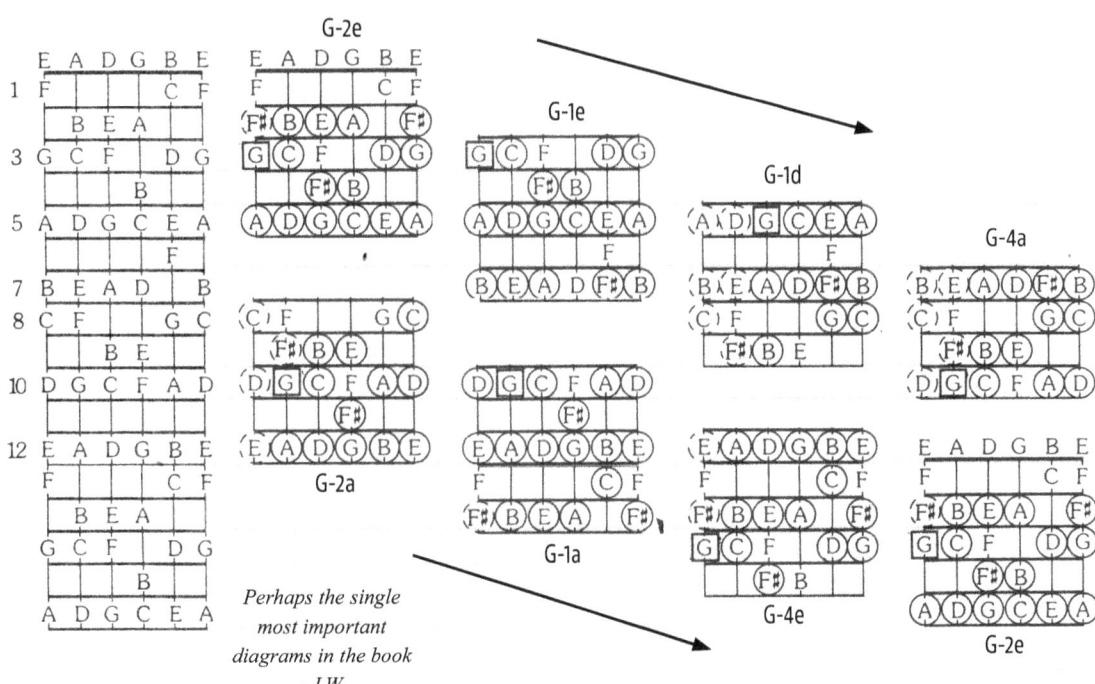

Perhaps the single most important diagrams in the book
- LW

Lesson 7

Applying Your Resources – The Major Scale

Now that you know a few of the major scale fingerings, where can you use them in your playing?

You can use the scale over any chord progression that is a progression *in* the key of the scale. For instance:

C Major Scale   C   D   E   F   G   A   B   C
                           I   ii   iii   IV   V   vi   vii

		Notes In The Chord	Chord Abbreviation
	C Major seventh	C E G B	Cma7
	D minor seventh	D F A C	Dmi7
The 4-note	E minor seventh	E G B D	Emi7
Diatonic Chords of	F Major seventh	F A C E	Fma7
the C Major Scale	G dominant seventh	G B D F	G7
	A minor seventh	A C E G	Ami7
	B minor seventh flat five	B D F A	Bmi7♭5

All of the above chords occur in the key of C Major. When you are playing in the key of C Major, you can play the notes of the C scale "over" any of these chords as you improvise. Below are some sample progressions that occur in the key of C Major. / means one beat and strum. ||: :|| are "Repeat signs." Whenever you see these two signs, repeat whatever is between them.

#1 ||:   Cma7   Cma7   Fma7   G7   :|| #2 ||:   Emi7   Ami7   Dmi7   G7   :||
                ////   ////   ////   ////   ////   ////   ////   ////

#3 ||:   Cma7   Dmi7   Emi7   Dmi7   :|| #4 ||:   Dmi7   G7   Cma7   Cma7   :||
                ////   ////   ////   ////   ////   ////   ////   ////

Use a backing track to play these chord changes so you can practice playing the scale over chords. For instance:

1. Start a short melody (or melodic pattern) with each note in the scale.
2. Try going up and down the scale with one melodic pattern, and then with several different ones - alternating or combining them together.
3. Try sliding into notes from one fret below (a useful "blues" tool). Don't be afraid of wrong notes at this point.
4. Try large interval leaps like a sixth, seventh or an octave, at the start of your improvised melody. (C to A?)
5. Play a little phrase and then try it over again one octave higher.
6. Try different rhythms. Really try and make it sound good. Play in any style you like, at an easy tempo. You are not trying to test yourself here, but to learn and have some fun.

Lesson 8

Examples of Melodies

Following are some examples of melodies created from the Diatonic Major scale.

The melodies are shown without rhythm, and are notated in the following manner:

1. The melodies will be given to you in a *specific scale fingering.*
2. Locate that fingering and play the scale several times before playing the "melody."
3. To play the melody, read and play the notes in the order they are numbered in the diagram.
4. PLAY at an even tempo. There are eight notes for each chord.

Play these over a backing track so you can hear the "melodies" against the chords. Play slowly and evenly. DON'T RUSH! These are just simple examples of how to take notes from the C Major scale, and build improvised sounds. These are not "the greatest solos ever played" sounds - you're trying to learn, and we are trying to show you the first steps (not impress or baffle you - that's book 2).

Position 2a - C Major

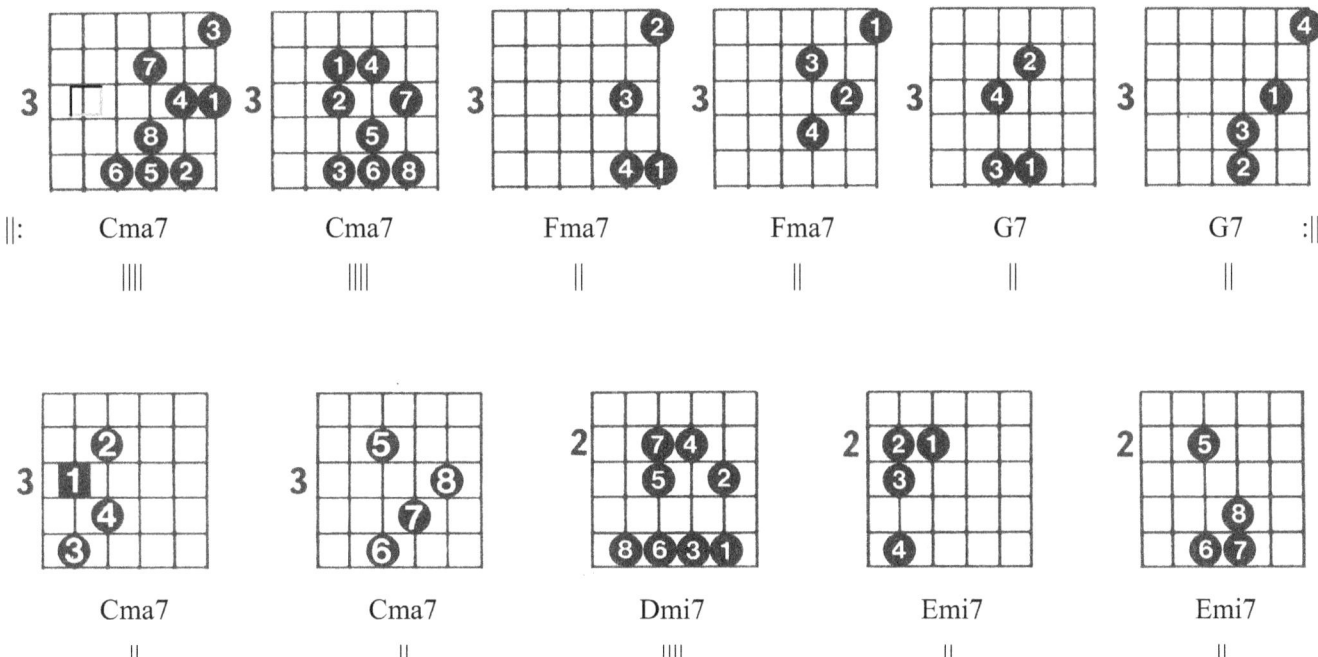

Position 2a - C Major

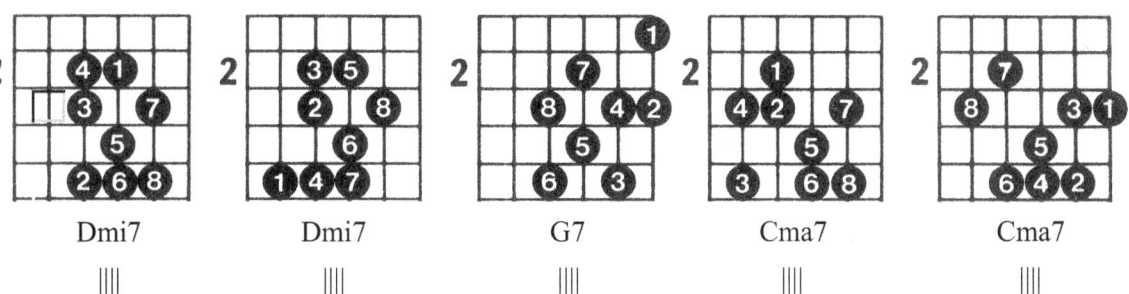

Position 4e   C Major

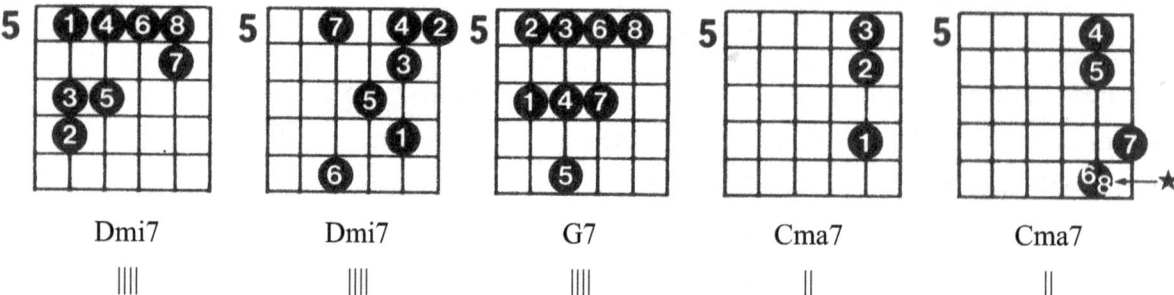

* This means that you should play this note twice. Once as the sixth note of the solo, and once as the eighth.

These sample "solos" have been given here to:
- Show how easy it can be to begin creating melodies out of scales and melodic patterns, and
- Suggest possible ideas for some of your own melodies. Patience and effort are the two keys to success here. You must work at it (and experiment).

The Importance of Melody

The better the melody you play, the better you sound. The melody (and your playing) HAVE to support the song. A melody must be recognizable. If it can be recognized, it can be remembered long enough for you to play a variation of it. That is how you construct longer meaningful solos. Joe Pass was one of the best at making interesting melodies even when he was playing very fast. I saw him repeatedly at Donte's in North Hollywood CA on Monday nights. I can remember the energy and soaring feeling he delivered. Incredible. And often on a tune like "Tea for Two."

The notion of "theme and variation" is universal to all forms of music from classical to great film scores, rock, blues, and country. Make a short melodic phrase and develop simple variations on it. You can add a note, change a note, change volume, or delay a note. Backing tracks can be helpful, but they should relate to songs you know or want to learn. Even in blues styles, imitate B.B King and deliver the *song,* not just licks.

Variation in Improvising

The album "John Mayall and the Blues Breakers featuring Eric Clapton" is a complete tutorial on making great solos for guitar. Hideaway (by Freddie King) is one of my favorites. Mr. Clapton (EC) uses rhythmic variation in every phrase to take a simple five note lick into incredible sounds. Memorizing that solo note-for-note is recommended. If you get that into your head you'll be able to draw upon many wonderful variations. Here are a few.

1. I gave you some melodic patterns that were 'straight eighths' ("one-and-two-and...") and triplets ("one-trip-let, two-trip-let"). This is an example of 3 vs 2 in feel. Try playing all the major scales in triplets (three notes per beat). Then try four notes per beat. Do that in your melodies. EC does.
2. Duration - Sometimes let the last note of a phrase ring, sometimes mute it with either hand, to make it short. Play a 4 note phrase with very short notes, and then notes of long duration. Again "Hideaway" is a master lesson.
3. Volume (and Snap) - Emphasizing a note by making it louder is a great way to make a phrase memorable.
4. String bends and vibrato - Adjusting the pitch of a note either by bending a string or changing your downward pressure in holding it can create powerful effects. The upcoming lesson on bends will show you how.
5. Space - welcoming silence into your improvisation is a little daunting at first, but allows you and the audience to breath in between phrases. It can add emphasis, allow you to change directions or feel, and let other instruments speak. Again "Hideaway" or "Little Girl" are great examples.
6. Above all else, try to be singing your melodies. Yes, most of us sound terrible so keep it soft. But your need to catch a breath is one of the best natural phrasing tools you have. Don't skip it.

Lesson 9

String Bends

Most lessons in technique have one thing in common. In general, technique is more difficult to explain than it is to understand or play. The best way for you to understand a discussion on technique is to play it, play it, and play it! Try everything - spend time "fooling around" - what is dry and long-winded on paper can turn into a real thrill on the guitar.

Because bending a string is raising (or lowering) a pitch, it can be done two ways - in tune (from one pitch to another) or out of tune (bending a note to some sound *between* two musical pitches - bending C to a note BETWEEN D# and E is an example of this.) You should learn to control your bending so that you can bend either way, when you want to. There is nothing worse than hearing a guitarist scream through a solo and bend a string to some horribly uncertain note! There are two basic physical motions involved in playing a note when you bend it.

1. Right hand: your right hand has the job of hitting the string (at the right time!) to sound the note.
2. Left hand: your left hand must push or pull the string out of its normal position; and pull it the right distance — to whatever pitch you want.

There can be tremendous variety in the sounds of string bending because there are various ways to time the picking of the note with the bend.

Below are shown the basic IN TUNE bend and pick combinations.

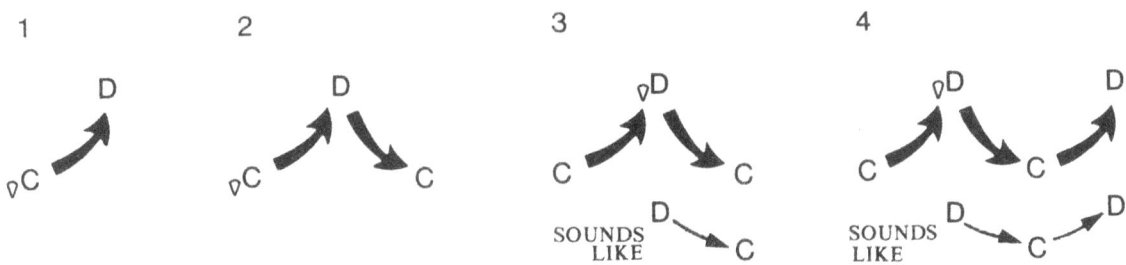

The ▽ symbol stands for the act of picking the string. The arrows signify whether you're going up or down in pitch. By "bending down" we mean slowly releasing a bent string back to its original pitch. Any time you push or pull a string out of its normal location, you're going to raise its pitch. However, if you pick the note after you have bent it (as far as you intend to) and then release the bend, the note will sound as if it's sliding DOWN (in pitch). See example 3 above.

There is one small problem here. Have you noticed it? How can you tell when you have bent the string far enough "up" if you haven't heard the note?? The answer is ... you can't, at first. If you play example (1) enough, your hand will remember how far it had to push to get the D note. Then when you do want to play example 3 successfully, your experience and the "feel" of where that D note is in the bend, will allow you to do so.

What is the difference, on paper, between examples 1 and 2? Where the sound *ends*.

In example # 1 it could end two ways: 1) by dying out on its own, 2) by being stopped deliberately - choked. The last sound is a D.

In example #2 you hang on to the string, and bring it back down to a C note.

Light gauge strings are advised for frequent string bending (string sets beginning with a .010, .09, or smaller, for the High E string, can be used EASILY by most players. The heavier gauged sets require more strength and/or practice. "Tens" - .010 to .046 are frequently shipped on new electric guitars. Jazz and acoustic really demand a beefier string. I alternate between "Elevens" and "Tens.")

Do you push up or pull down? Yes. Except for the high E string which you can only push up, you'll find that you push up and pull down at various times, which depends on how you feel, what feels "good" to you at that time, and what sound you're looking for.

How you bend is largely a matter of personal taste. It's up to you to experiment.

3. SPECIAL NOTE*** - When bending strings, *how* do you push up the string? It is better to push the string up with the tip of your finger (see picture). When pulling a string towards the floor, the fleshy pad of the finger does the job the best (see picture). Try it, and you'll see.
4. Where can we bend strings? What intervals in the scale (or out) work??

For our discussion here, we will only consider bends in the major scale. Typically the easiest finger to bend with is the third finger. The next easiest is the 4th. So, look at each fingering shape, and see which notes are under the third and fourth fingers. Those will be a good place to start.

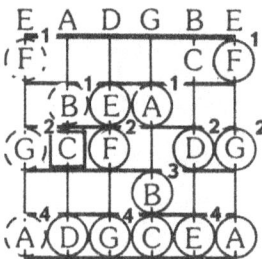

Let's look at fingering C-2a (shown to the left). If we consider bending on the three highest strings only, for the moment, and favor our third and fourth fingers, we've got several good options.

On the third string, bend the B note (3rd finger) up to the C note - a 1/2 step bend.

The second easy bend is the E note on the second string. Again, this is a half step bend so bend the E note up to the F note.

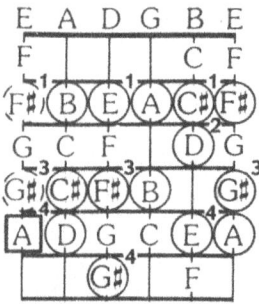

This A-4e fingering demonstrates several important ideas. Play the scale to get the sound in your ear and then try the following bends:

On the third string bend the B note up a whole step to a C# note (3rd finger).

On the second string, bend the E note up to an F# note (4th finger).

Now try something different: place your 4th finger on the 1st string A note and hold it there. Place your 3rd finger on the E note on the second string. Striking both strings at once, hold the A note, and bend the E note. That should give you a nice country sounding lick.

Keeping your 4th finger on the A note (1st string), use your 3rd finger to bend the B note on the third string. You should get another nice country sound.

A simple bend motion can give you a LOT of sounds. The key is to LISTEN and apply variations. Bending the E note in the A-4e fingering is a simple enough thing to do. BUT, adding the higher A note as a pedal (a sustaining note) gives it a new sound, and a different fingering.

Diving in to detail, you can hit both strings at once and then bend, or hit one string and then the other (in either order) and bend. OR you could change the rhythm of the bend (when you hit each note in relation to the beat), and even change how long you hold the notes. Imitating a pedal steel suggests you let the notes sustain, but you can also choke them so they're very short. (Let your fingers up, but *not off* the strings.)

As you saw above, we had you hold TWO pedals (the A and E notes) and bend the B note on the third string. Although you're adjusting your fingering, it gets the job done. Try NOT playing the E note in that set - just the outside two notes. Pick, bend up, hold, and bend down. Then just pick and bend up.

You may have to be thinking about it all now, but this will become second nature after some playing. Just make sure you explore all the options and remain aware of what you or other players can do. Knowing what you're hearing will help give you lots of ideas for your own playing.

Lesson 10

Preparing for Arpeggios - Chords and Degrees

The capital Roman Numerals are the MAJOR sounding chords. The small Roman numerals are the MINOR sounding chords. This kind of notation is a shorthand when referring to chords found in the scale. If you look for three note chords (triads), the major triads (like G major) are found on the 1st, 4th, and 5th degrees of the major scale. Minor triads are found on the 2nd, 3rd, and 6th degrees.

When you look at FOUR note chords found in the scale, things take a twist. The chords found on the 1st and 4th degrees are *major* sevenths, but the 5th degree chord is a *dominant* seventh. Compare the triads and four note chords in the table below. (It uses the G major Scale, like the first arpeggio group.) In this book we'll typically use the Roman numerals to refer to the four note chords, but not the triads.

	TRIADS				4 NOTE CHORDS		
Name	Spelling	Chord Symbol		Spelling	Chord Symbol	Name	
G Major	G B D	G	I	G B D F#	Gma7	G Major seventh
A minor	A C E	Amin	ii	A C E G	Ami7	A minor seventh
B minor	B D F#	Bmin	iii	B D F# A	Bmi7	B minor seventh
C Major	C E G	C	IV	C E G B	Cma7	C Major seventh
D Major	D F# A	D	V	D F# A C	D7	D dominant seventh
E minor	E G B	Emin	vi	E G B D	Emi7	E minor seventh
F# diminished	F# A C	F#dim	vii	F# A C E	F#mi7b5	F# minor seventh flat five

Why do we care about the chord spellings? As we said before, arpeggios are the notes of the chords played one at a time. They are spelled with the same notes. Thus we're learning to connect the sounds of the chords with melodic improvisation using the same notes.

Chord Names and Symbols

Various shorthand symbols are used to indicate chords. Shown below are common chords and their shorthand names.

C Major Seventh	CMA7, Cma7, CM7, Cmaj7, C△7
C Minor Seventh	Cmi7, Cmin7
C Dominant Seventh	C7
C Dominant Eleventh	C11
C "nine" (Dominant Ninth)	C9
C Minor Seventh flat five	Cmin7♭5, Cmi7♭5, Cø7 ("C half diminished"), Cmi7-5, Cmin7-5
C Seven Sharp Nine	C7#9, C7+9
A Minor Thirteenth	Amin13, AMin13, Ami13
G Nine Sharp Eleven	G9#11, G9+11
B11 Flat Nine	B11♭9, B11-9
C Diminished Seventh	Co7, Cdim7, CDim7

The Roman numerals are also a bit of a code. Capital Roman numerals generally mean a Major sound (the I, IV, V) while small Roman numerals refer to minor chords (ii, iii, iv). However some musicians use 'caps' for all Roman numerals as they assume you know a ii chord is minor.

Lesson 11

The Arpeggio

Scales have notes close together (usually a half step or whole step apart; that is, one or two frets apart).

Arpeggios are chords played one note at a time. More importantly, they have *larger* intervals between the notes.

We have been using scales to teach your ear the small interval sounds. We will use the arpeggios to teach your ear large interval sounds. The arpeggio is a bridge between scales and chords. With its larger jumps it also covers more strings more quickly than a scale, so playing arpeggios is a great way to improve your picking technique.

Each of the scale fingerings you've seen contain seven arpeggios for the basic four note chords found in the scale.

In essence, we'll revisit each fingering and learn seven different ways to play through it. Each arpeggio outlines a particular 4 note chord found in that scale.

1. Remember that all these arpeggio fingerings are based on our major scale fingerings, so there should be NO CONFUSION!
2. We are going to study the arpeggios as they occur from each of our scale fingerings. We will take one scale position at a time, and thoroughly explore all the arpeggios of the chords in that "key" position before continuing. (If this is not clear, reread Lesson 6.)
3. *Many of the arpeggio fingerings repeat in other keys and scale fingerings.* You will see the same Emi7 arpeggio fingering in the keys of C, G and D. (Yes, we're cheating sort of.)
4. The study of arpeggios is very important, and a lot of fun. Take your time, work carefully, always use alternate picking and remember, remain seated till we come to a complete stop and the captain has turned off the "No Playing" sign.
5. If you would like to improve your picking technique, try the following ideas as you explore the arpeggios:
- Begin your alternate picking of an arpeggio on an "up" stroke, rather than a "down" stroke.
- Play each note of the arpeggio twice instead of just once. Use alternate picking and then reverse it.
6. Play each note of the arpeggio three times, using alternate picking.

Special Notation

A *circle* indicates a note in the arpeggio

A *square* indicates the Root of an arpeggio

A *broken* circle shows a note in the arpeggio, but *below the Root* (it is optional at this point).

Let's look at the diagram below. Place your hand in the G-2e major scale position. The arpeggio illustrated here is in the same position.

The circled notes belong to the Gma7 arpeggio. Start on the low G (the Root) and play up the arpeggio. Which fingers do you use?? Use the fingering you normally would for position 2e.

Repeat this arpeggio up and down several times. Since these notes are part of the 2e scale fingering, and you know that fingering, you should not have to look at your guitar to play this.

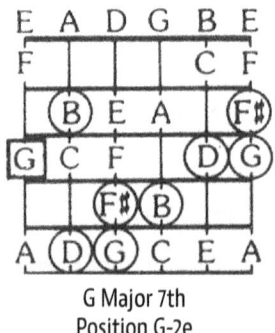

G Major 7th
Position G-2e

Lesson 12

Arpeggio Group #1 - G Major 2e Fingering

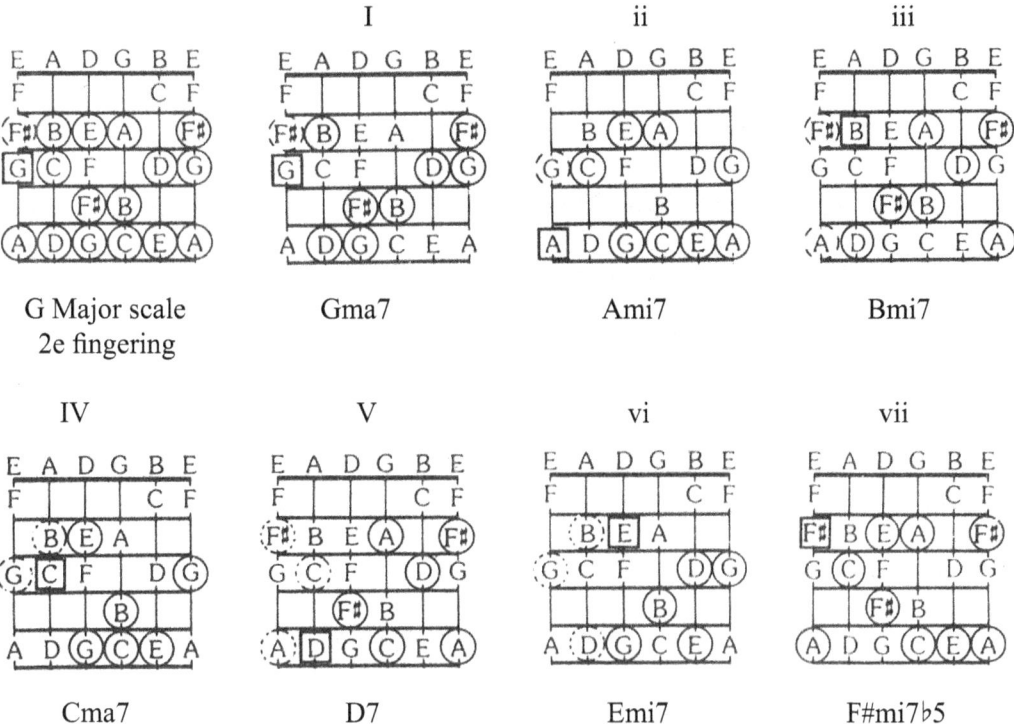

Shown above is the position 2e fingering for the G Major scale, and the seven diatonic arpeggios in the key of G Major.

- There is one arpeggio for each four note chord in the key.
- The names of the chords and arpeggios are written underneath each diagram.
- The Roman numeral above each arpeggio diagram indicates the degree of the major scale from which the arpeggio is built.

The notes of the scale:	G	A	B	C	D	E	F# G
The degrees of the scale	I	ii	iii	IV	V	vi	vii

Learning Arpeggios

1. Memorize the arpeggios shown above in this order: I, ii, iii, IV, V, vi, vii. To memorize the arpeggio, play it slowly, ascending and descending.

2. The "Roll Technique:" Look at this Ami7 arpeggio fingering. Try it. Can you see the problem of the C and E notes (3rd and 2nd strings) played by the fourth finger? To play these two notes on the same fret, and on adjacent strings, ROLL your fourth finger from one string to the next (see sketch). This roll is used frequently in other situations as well, so begin to learn it now.

3. In general all our arpeggio diagrams will show a two octave arpeggio. (From F up to the next F is one octave; as is G to G, C# to C# and so on - a two octave arpeggio would be F to F to F as shown here.)

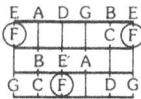

The octaves of F are circled

1. Try to practice all of the arpeggios in two octaves. You'll find the rhythm and picking will work out better. In our first arpeggio position you can play the Gma7 arpeggio, G up to G; the Ami7 arpeggio, A to A.
2. However, the Bmi7 arpeggio cannot be played B to B in this position, as shown. Since the highest possible note in this Bmi7 arpeggio position is A, hold one or two of the notes longer, when necessary, to give yourself a rhythm you can remember.
3. Use alternate picking throughout all of these exercises. Down on the first note, up on the second. When comfortable that way, reverse it by starting on an UP stroke first.
4. Once you are familiar with all seven arpeggios, practice them with the following progressions. These progressions were chosen because they appear (in whole or in part) in thousands of songs, in all styles of contemporary music. (Play each arpeggio ascending and descending before playing the next arpeggio.)

   a) ii V I; Ami7 - D7 - Gma7   **b) IV V I**; Cma7 - D7 - Gma7   **c) I ii iii ii;** Gma7 - Ami7 - Bmi7 - Ami7

   d) I vi IV V; Gma7 - Bmi7 - Cma7 - D7   **e) iii vi ii V I;** Emi7 - Bmi7 - Ami7 - D7 - Gma7

   f) IV vii iii vi ii V I; Cma7 - F#mi7b5 - Emi7 - Bmi7 - Ami7 - D7 - Gma7

5. Cut the examples in Step 4 above, in half. Play the first arpeggio ascending, the second one descending, the third ascending, and so on; then reverse that. Play the first arpeggio descending, the second ascending, and so on. It is very important that you master these exercises. Don't skip them!!
6. If you want further help in mastering the arpeggios, play up the arpeggio, and down the G scale; then up the next arpeggio, and down the scale, and continue through the progressions in #3 above. Reverse this too - play up the scale and down the arpeggio, or down the arpeggio and up the scale. Mixing arpeggios and scales was suggested by virtuoso Guitarist Johnny Smith.

Arpeggios can take a little while to be comfortable with – you have alternate picking across strings, left hand finger rolls, and more. Be patient here too.

Watch the page and let your EARS check and tell you when you're wrong. This will really improve your awareness of the notes and their sounds. Try singing the arpeggios as you play them ... (Virginia's father put on his earmuffs and waited for her wails to begin. "Whales?").

The Fork in the Road

Now that you've had a taste of arpeggios you have some options on how you can proceed through the rest of the book:

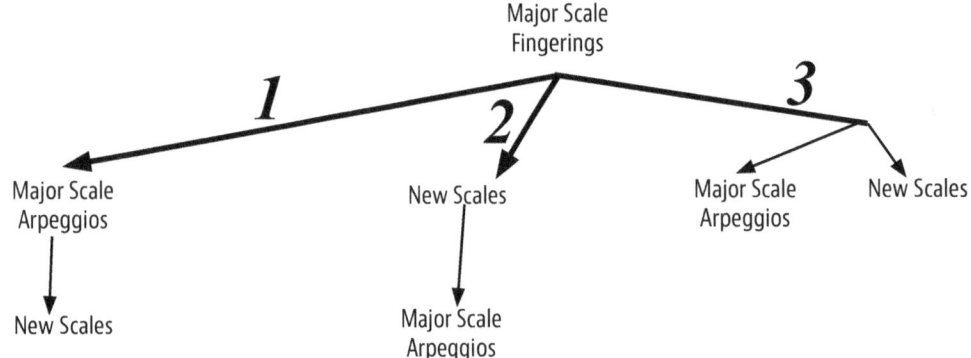

You can

1) continue working in the major scale sounds (including arpeggios) which prepares you for jazz soloing as well, or

2) leave the major scale sounds and move to the new scales like the pentatonics, or

3) work through both areas at the same time. I recommend doing the arpeggios first as the arpeggios set you up for all the remaining scales (if you remember the end of the "Introduction").

Lesson 13

Arpeggio Group #2 – A Major Scale 4e Fingering

This is our second arpeggio position. It is based upon the 4e scale fingering for the key of A major and includes the seven diatonic four note arpeggios in the key of A Major.

> The notes of the scale: A B C♯ D E F♯ G♯
> The degrees of the scale   I ii iii IV V vi vii

- There is one arpeggio for each four note chord in the key.
- The names of the chords and arpeggios are written underneath each diagram.
- The Roman numeral above each arpeggio diagram indicates the degree of the major scale.
- Proceed here as before.

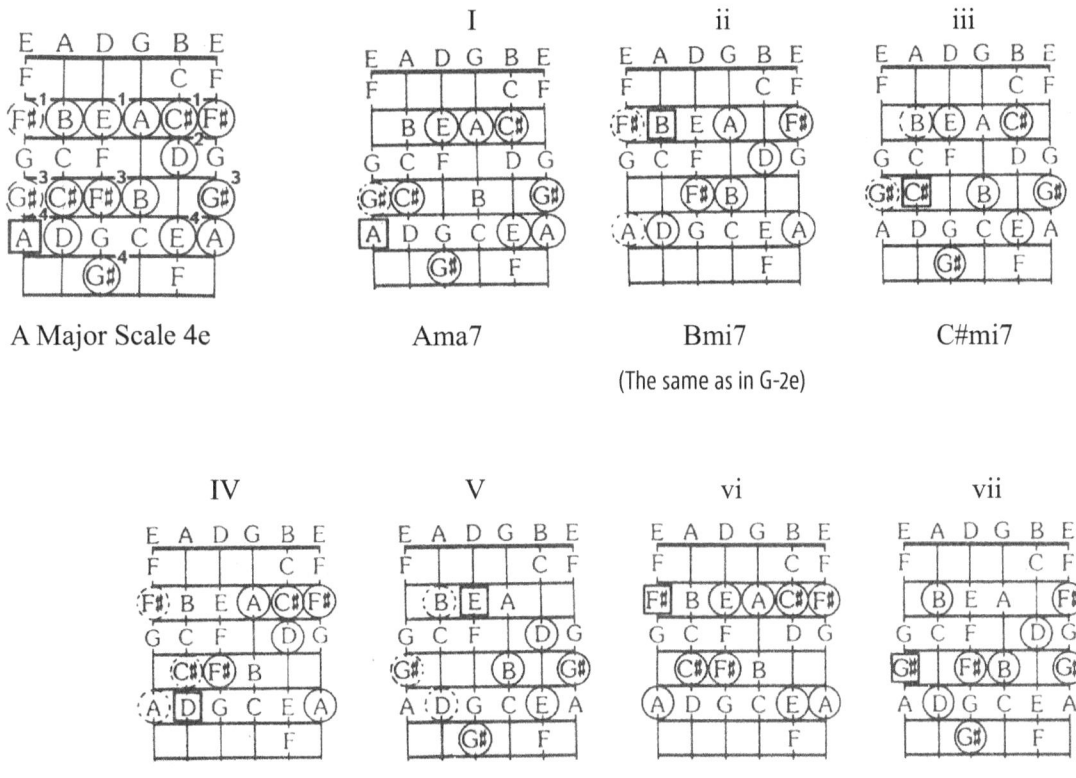

1. Memorize the arpeggios in this order: I, ii, iii, IV, V, vi, vii. (This is the order they are presented above.)
2. Play each arpeggio ascending and descending and then play the next arpeggio.
3. Use the arpeggios in these groups:
   a) ii V I; Bmi7 - E7 - Ama7   **b) I IV V I;** Ama7 - Dma7 - E7 - Ama7
   c) I ii iii ii; Ama7 - Bmi7 - C♯mi7 - Bmi7   **d) I vi IV V;** Ama7 - Dma7 - E7 - Ama7
   e) iii vi ii V I; C♯mi7 - F♯mi7 - Bmi7 - E7 - Ama7
   f) IV vii iii vi ii V I; Dma7 - G♯mi7b5 - C♯mi7 - F♯mi7 - Bmi7 - E7 - Ama7.

(The Roman letters are really important. You'll hear players speak about playing over a "iii-vi-ii-V "for example.)

1. Play exercise #3 but play UP one arpeggio and DOWN the next.
2. Reverse #4 and play down the first and up the second arpeggio.
3. Play up an arpeggio and then down the A Major scale. Then move to the next arpeggio for each of the examples in step #3 above. Each chord should receive four beats.

A Quick Arpeggio Review

Below is a simple chord progression shown with arpeggios from the *two* arpeggio positions we have seen so far. The rhythm of the "melodies" that these arpeggios will create is entirely up to you. In general, if you play two notes for each beat in a measure (that's eight notes in a measure of 4/4) you'll come out OK. If you reach the end of an arpeggio and need more notes, simply start to play back the arpeggio.

Take your time here. The purpose of this example is to help you think with arpeggios, as you *locate* them. The beats are shown below the chords. The fingerings are shown below the beats.

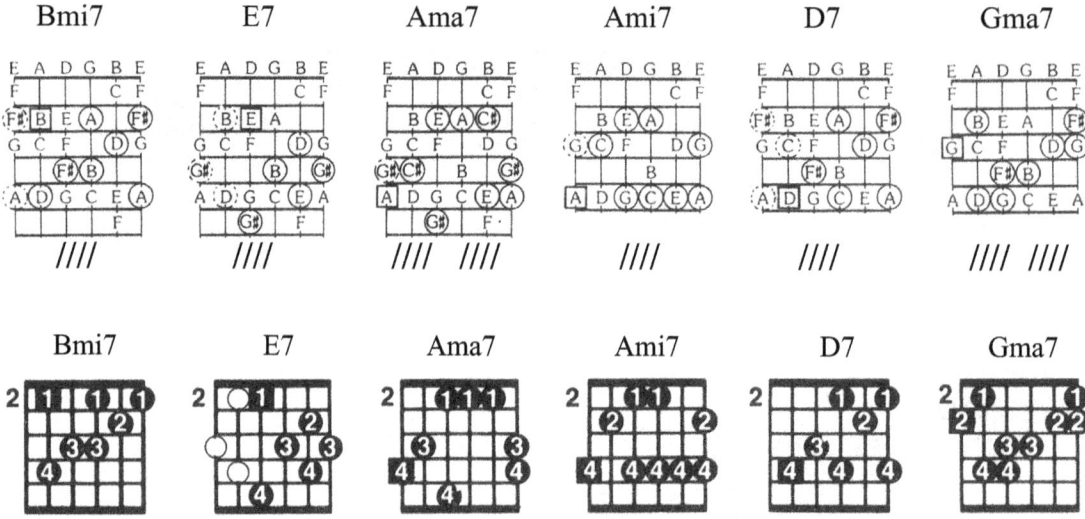

Try to play arpeggios over the following example. Only the chord names are given. Give each chord name 4 beats here. The progression is repeated.

Bmi7   E7   Ami7   D7   Gma7   Gma7   Bmi7   E7   Ami7   D7   Gma7   Gma7

This is often the way you'll see chord progressions for songs written out for jams and other 'casual' situations where you may be expected to know the tune. I left some room for you to write around the chords.

Lesson 14

Arpeggio Group #3 - F Major Scale 4a Fingering

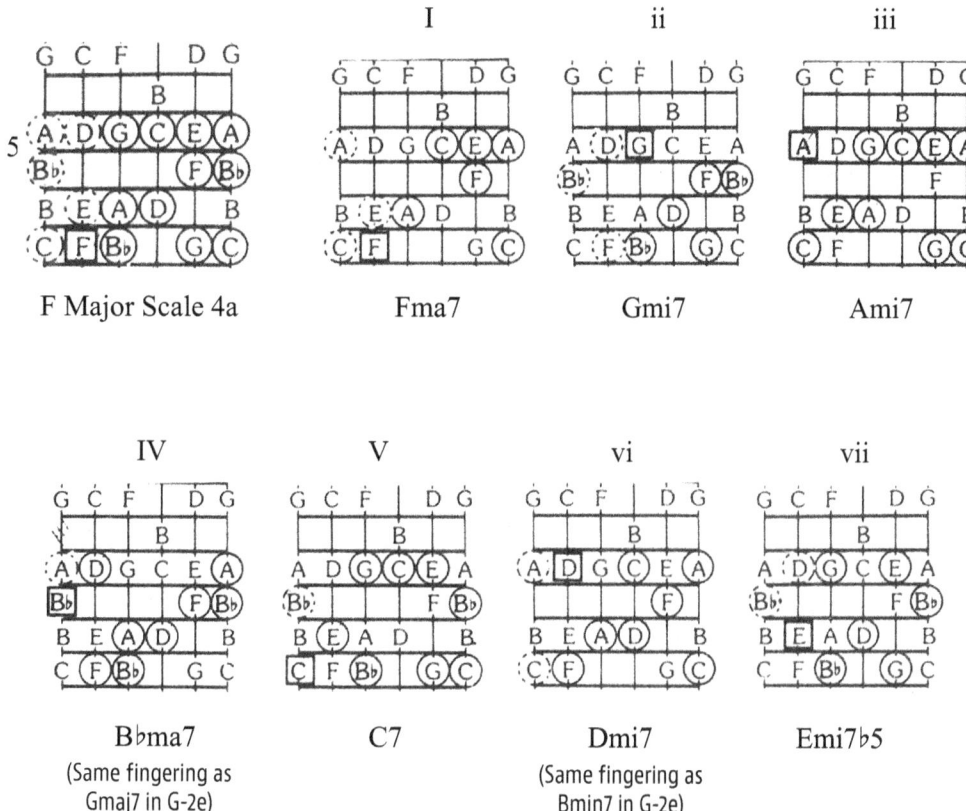

1. The F major scale fingering 4a is shown above with the arpeggios.

2. Memorize the arpeggios in this order: I, ii, iii, IV, V, vi, vii.

3. Play the arpeggios ascending and descending.

4. Use the arpeggios in these groups:

    a) ii V I;   Gmi7 - C7 - Fma7   b) I IV V I;   Fma7 - Bbma7 - C7 - Fma7

    c) I ii iii ii; Fma7 - Gmi7 - Ami7 - Gmi7   d) I vi IV V;   Fma7 - Dmi7 - Bbma7 - C7

    e) iii vi ii V I;   Ami7 - Dmi7 - Gmi7 - C7 - Fma7

    f) IV vii iii vi ii V I;   Bbma7 - Emi7b5 - Ami7 - Dmi7 - Gmi7 - C7 - Fma7

5. Play exercise #3 but play UP one arpeggio and DOWN the next.

6. Reverse #4 and play down the first and up the second arpeggio.

7. Note that the Bbmaj7 arpeggio is the same fingering here as the Gmaj7th arpeggio in fingering G2e. This Dmin7 arpeggio is the same pattern as the Bmin7 arpeggio in G2e. Do you see any other fingerings that are duplicated?

Lesson 15

Arpeggio Group #4 - C Major Scale 2a Fingering

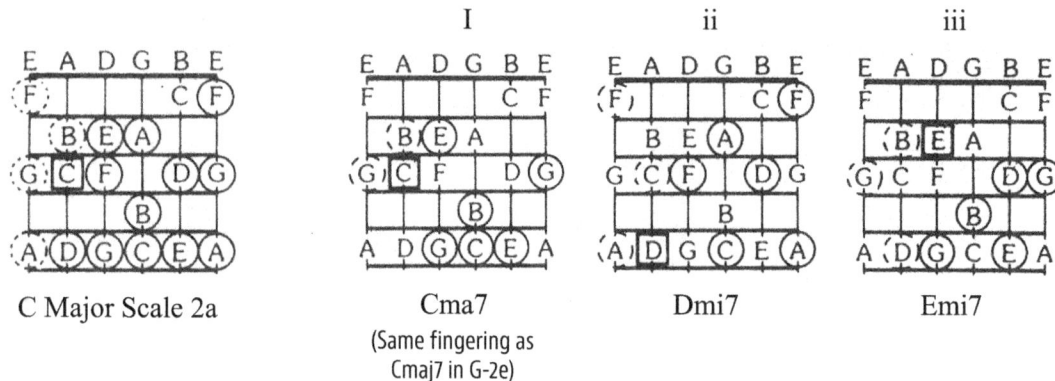

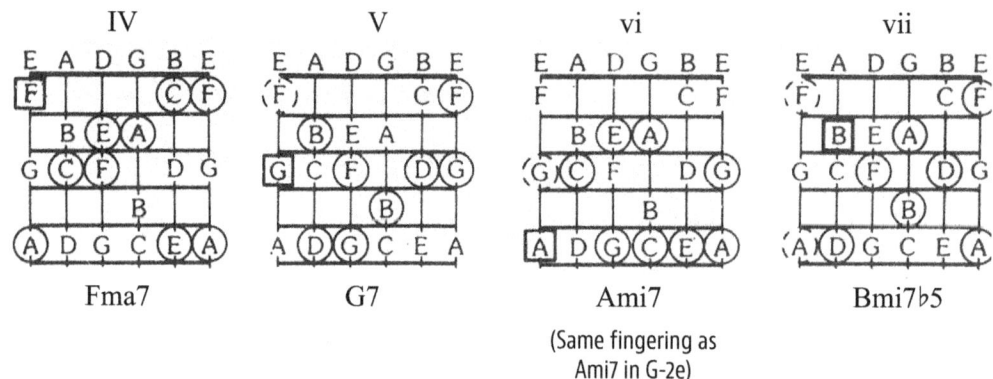

1. Memorize the arpeggios in this order: I, ii, iii, IV, V, vi, vii.

2. Play the arpeggios ascending and descending.

3. Use the arpeggios in these groups:

   a) ii V I; Dmi7 - G7 - Cma7   **b) I IV V I;** Cma7 - Fma7 - G7 - Cma7

   c) I ii iii ii; Cma7 - Dmi7 - Emi7 - Dmi7   **d) I vi IV V;** Cma7 - Ami7 - Fma7 - G7

   e) iii vi ii V I; Emi7 - Ami7 - Dmi7 - G7 - Cma7

   f) IV vii iii vi ii V I; Fma7 - Bmi7b5 - Emi7 - Ami7 - Dmi7 - G7 - Cma7

4. Play exercise #3 but play UP one arpeggio and DOWN the next.

5. Reverse #4 and play down the first and up the second arpeggio.

6. Now alternate between the scale of the key, and each arpeggio - play down the first arpeggio and up the scale, then down the second arpeggio and up that scale. Do this for the arpeggios presented in the examples of Step #3 above.

7. Reverse Step #6. Play down the scale and up the arpeggio (just the opposite of what you were doing). We cannot over-emphasize how important these arpeggio-scale exercises are. DO NOT SKIP THEM. The more you practice them, the less time it will take to learn new ones. You should be beginning to hear some interesting "lines" by now. Which arpeggio fingerings have you seen before?

Lesson 16

Arpeggio Key Group #5 – G Major Scale 1d Fingering

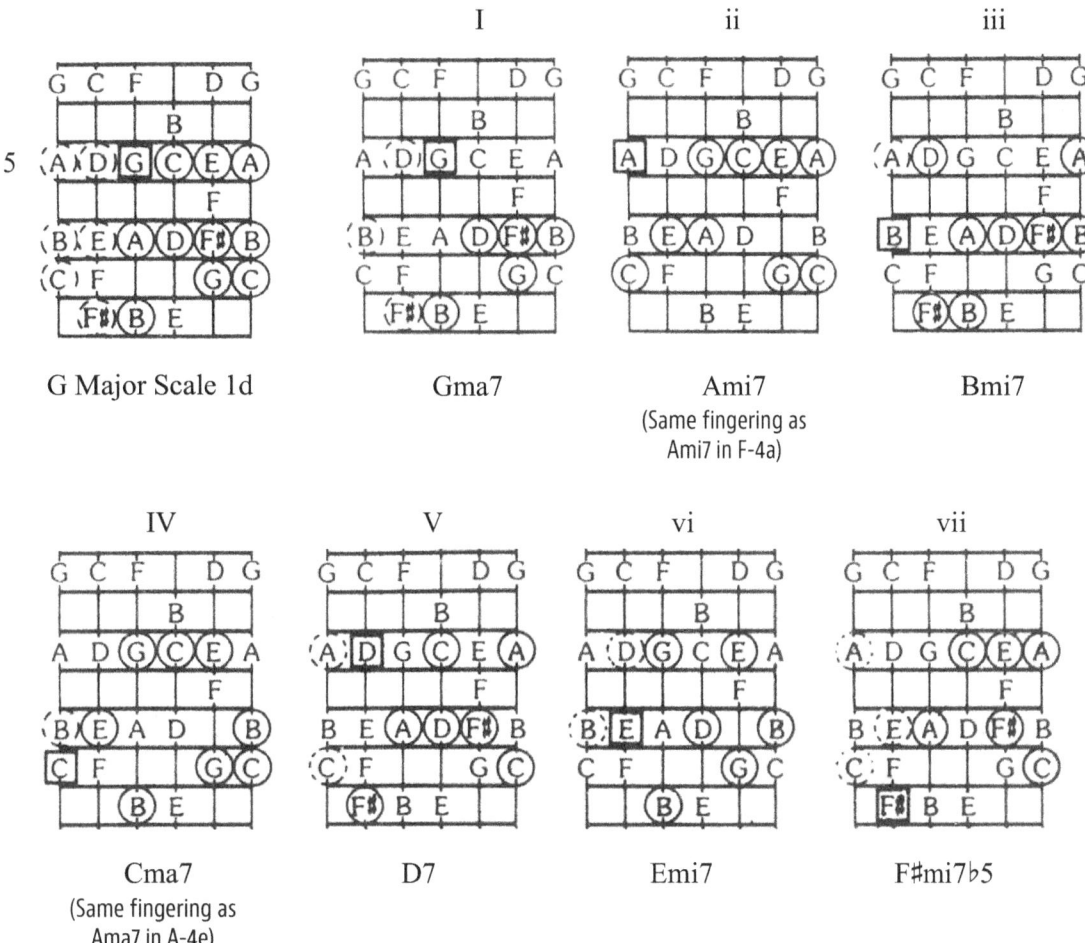

This position is in the key of G major. It has the same arpeggio sounds as our first position, but with fingerings based on the fingering position 1d. Memorize these fingerings and proceed as before, through the progressions.

1. Memorize the arpeggios in this order: I, ii, iii, IV, V, vi, vii.

2. Play the arpeggios ascending and descending.

3. Use the arpeggios in these groups:

   a) ii V I; Ami7 - D7 - Gma7   **b) I IV V I;** Gma7 - Cma7 - D7 - Gma7

   c) I ii iii ii; Gma7 - Ami7 - Bmi7 - Ami7   **d) I vi IV V;** Gma7 - Emi7 - Cma7 - D7

   e) iii vi ii V I; Bmi7 - Emi7 - Ami7 - D7 - Gma7

   f) IV vii iii vi ii V I; Cma7 - F#mi7b5 - Bmi7 - Emi7 - Ami7 - D7 - Gma7

4. Play exercise #3 but play up one arpeggio and DOWN the next.

5. Reverse #4 and play down the first and up the second arpeggio.

6. Compare the arpeggio fingerings of this group with the first group of arpeggios.

7. Remember, all the arpeggio fingerings are contained inside the major scale fingerings you've already learned. Look for familiar arpeggio fingerings.

Lesson 17

Arpeggio Key Group #6 – F Major Scale 1a

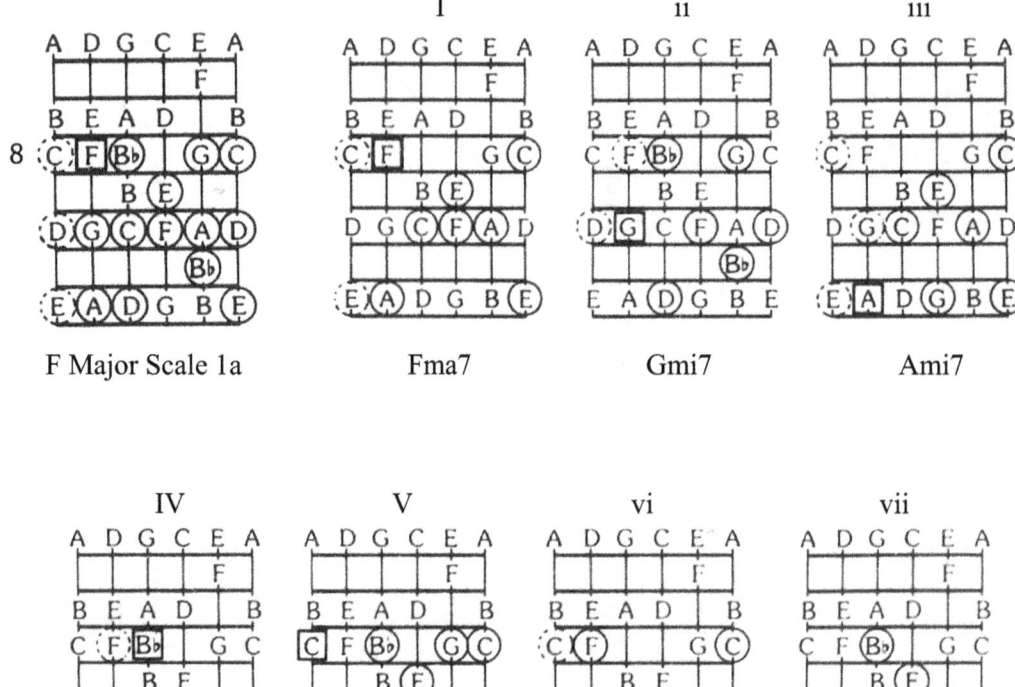

This arpeggio fingering group is based on the F major scale 1a fingering.

1. Memorize the arpeggios in this order: I, ii, iii, IV, V, vi, vii.

2. Play the arpeggios ascending and descending.

3. Use the arpeggios in these groups:

   a) ii V I; Gmi7 - C7 - Fma7   **b) I IV V I;** Fma7 - Bbma7 - C7 - Fma7

   c) I ii iii ii; Fma7 - Gmi7 - Ami7 - Gmi7   **d) I vi IV V;** Fma7 - Dmi7 - Bbma7 - C7

   e) iii vi ii V I; Ami7 - Dmi7 - Gmi7 - C7 - Fma7

   f) IV vii iii vi ii V I; Bbma7 - Emi7b5 - Ami7 - Dmi7 - Gmi7 - C7 - Fma7

4. Play exercise #3 but play UP one arpeggio and DOWN the next.

5. Reverse #4 and play down the first and up the second arpeggio.

6. Now alternate between the scale of the key, and each arpeggio - play down the first arpeggio and up the scale, then down the second arpeggio and up that scale. Do this for the arpeggios presented in the examples of #3, above.

7. Reverse Step #6. Play down the scale and up the arpeggio (just the opposite of what you were doing).

8. It should be easy to recognize familiar fingerings by now. . .

Lesson 18

Arpeggio Key Group #7 - F Major Scale 1e Fingering

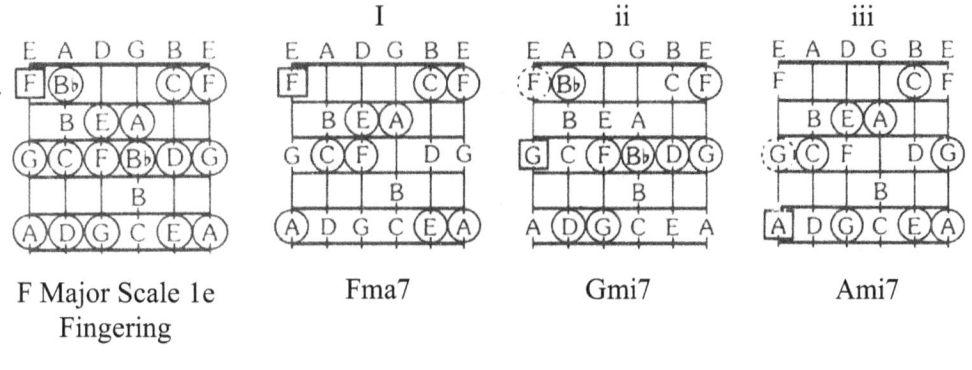

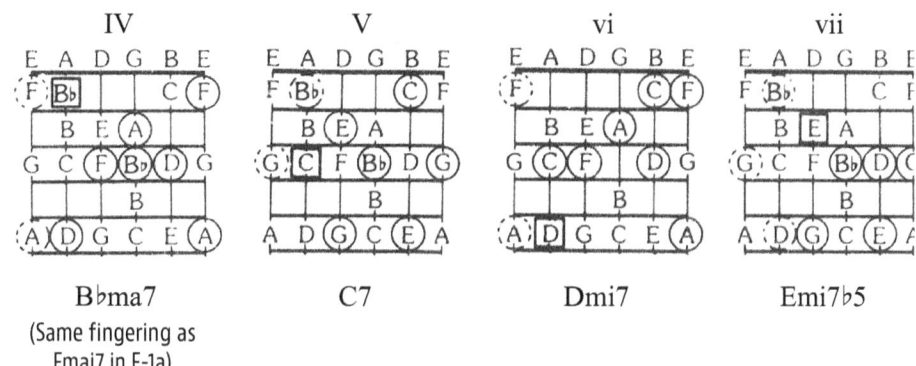

1. Memorize the arpeggios in this order: I, ii, iii, IV, V, vi, vii.

2. Play the arpeggios ascending and descending.

3. Use the arpeggios in these groups:

    a) ii V I; Gmi7 - C7 - Fma7
    b) I IV V I; Fma7 - B♭ma7 - C7 - Fma7
    c) I ii iii ii; Fma7 - Gmi7 - Ami7 - Gmi7
    d) I vi IV V; Fma7 - Dmi7 - B♭ma7 - C7
    e) iii vi ii V I; Ami7 - Dmi7 - Gmi7 - C7 - Fma7
    f) IV vii iii vi ii V I; B♭ma7 - Emi7♭5 - Ami7 - Dmi7 - Gmi7 - C7 - Fma7

4. Play exercise #3 but play UP one arpeggio and DOWN the next.

5. Reverse #4 and play down the first and up the second arpeggio.

6. Play up an arpeggio and down the scale, for each arpeggio in each progression in #3 above.

By now you are either getting very good at arpeggios (and you're starting to put them in your own solos) or you are very tired of arpeggios. If you're in the second group, why don't you work in another area for a while and then come back to these arpeggios later? A little more time and experience will probably clear this up for you. Don't be concerned!!

Lesson 19 Part A

Arpeggio Review by Scale Fingering

Below is a complete listing of the seven arpeggio key-scale fingering positions. Check yourself here. Can you play through all the positions? Which positions are your favorites?

	I	ii	iii	IV	V	vi	vii
2e G Major	Gma7	Ami7	Bmi7	Cma7	D7	Emi7	F#mi7♭5
4e A Major	Ama7	Bmi7	C#mi7	Dma7	E7	F#mi7	G#mi7♭5
4a F Major	Fma7	Gmi7	Ami7	B♭ma7	C7	Dmi7	Emi7♭5
2a C Major	Cma7	Dmi7	Emi7	Fma7	G7	Ami7	Bmi7♭5
1d G Major	Gma7	Ami7	Bmi7	Cma7	D7	Emi7	F#mi7♭5
1a F Major	Fma7	Gmi7	Ami7	B♭ma7	C7	Dmi7	Emi7♭5
1e F Major	Fma7	Gmi7	Ami7	B♭ma7	C7	Dmi7	Emi7♭5

Styles for the Studio by Leon White

Lesson 19 Part B

Arpeggio Review by Fingering Shape

This page is also a review of all the arpeggios you have seen. The arpeggios are listed according to their common root fingering. If you look down the "1e" column, you'll see the Major seventh, dominant seventh, minor seventh, and minor seventh flat five arpeggios from the common fingering position "1e." This holds true as you read down each of the other columns that illustrate the other fingering positions.

Play down each column and listen to the difference in sound. Knowing different sounds from the same location is important when you are playing songs with changes in tonal centers. In the example, immediately following, you can see that you'll be playing two different arpeggios from the same root.

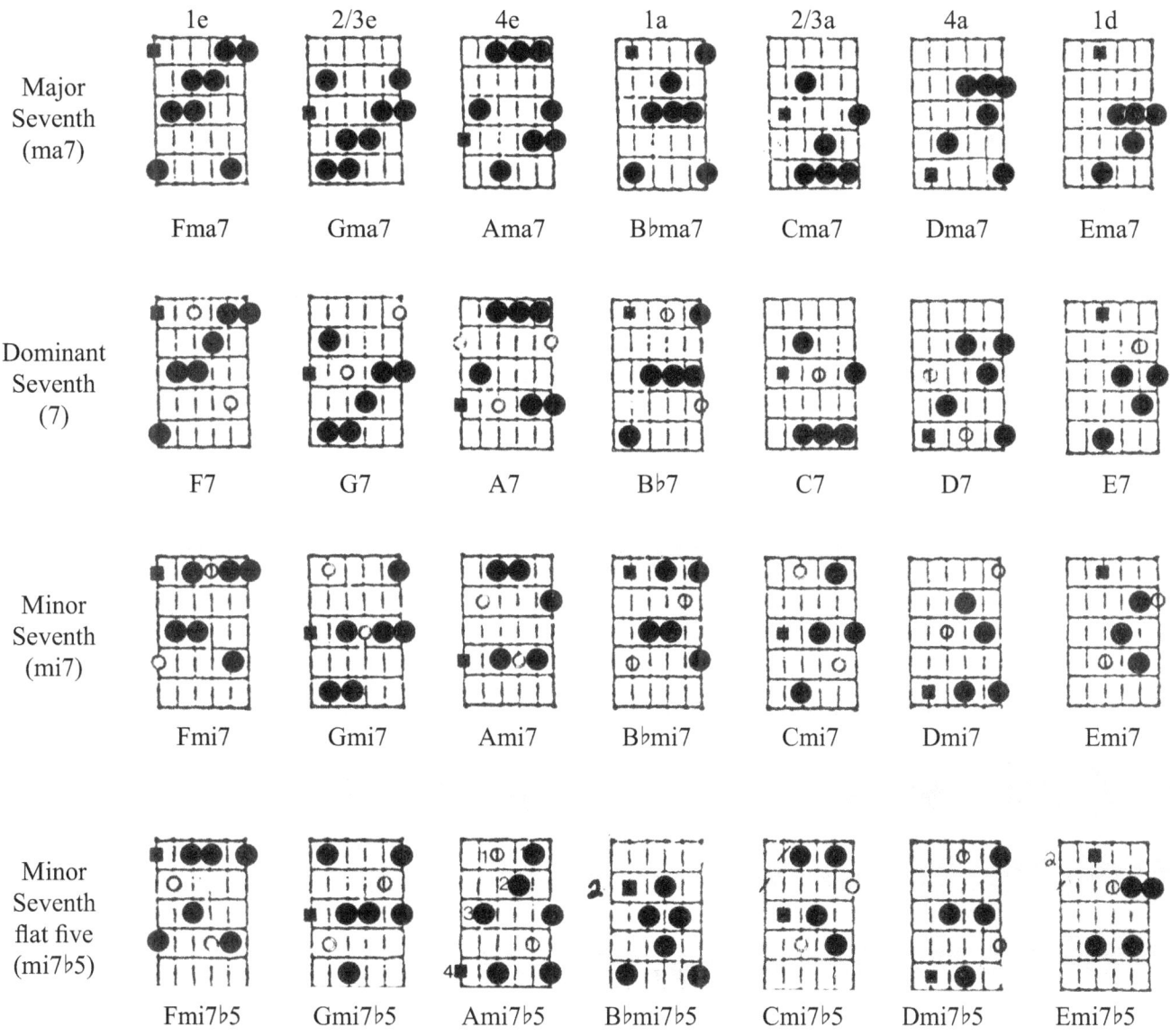

Watch your fingering!

Lesson 20
Arpeggio Review - Usage

Finger Facility

The following steps below may feel like the "play it in all 12 keys" you read in instructions books or hear teachers say. All seriousness aside, the more time you spend moving through the arpeggios the better you'll improvise.

1. In your first arpeggio positions play the I chord arpeggio ascending and the Major scale descending. Repeat this for each arpeggio in the position in this order: I ii iii IV V vi vii. (This is the Johnny Smith suggestion.)
2. Reverse the above - play the scale ascending and then descend with the arpeggios.
3. Try either or both of Steps A and B in chord progressions you are familiar with. For instance - ii V I or I IV V I.
4. Proceed through Steps 1-3 above for each of the seven arpeggio positions. Take one position a week and try it for thirty minutes a day if you can. As you complete this for each fingering position, you will be amazed at your increasing command of the fingerboard.

Reviewing and Connecting Fingering Positions

The following examples are given to help you:
- See how one progression could be dealt with in more than one position; and to
- See how to connect the positions together for chord progressions that involve more than one tonal center, or involve chords NOT in the original key.

The examples below are each a simple chord progression with several different arpeggio key groups for you to play. Experiment. Take any progression in any key and see how many fingerings you can use to play the arpeggio sounds.

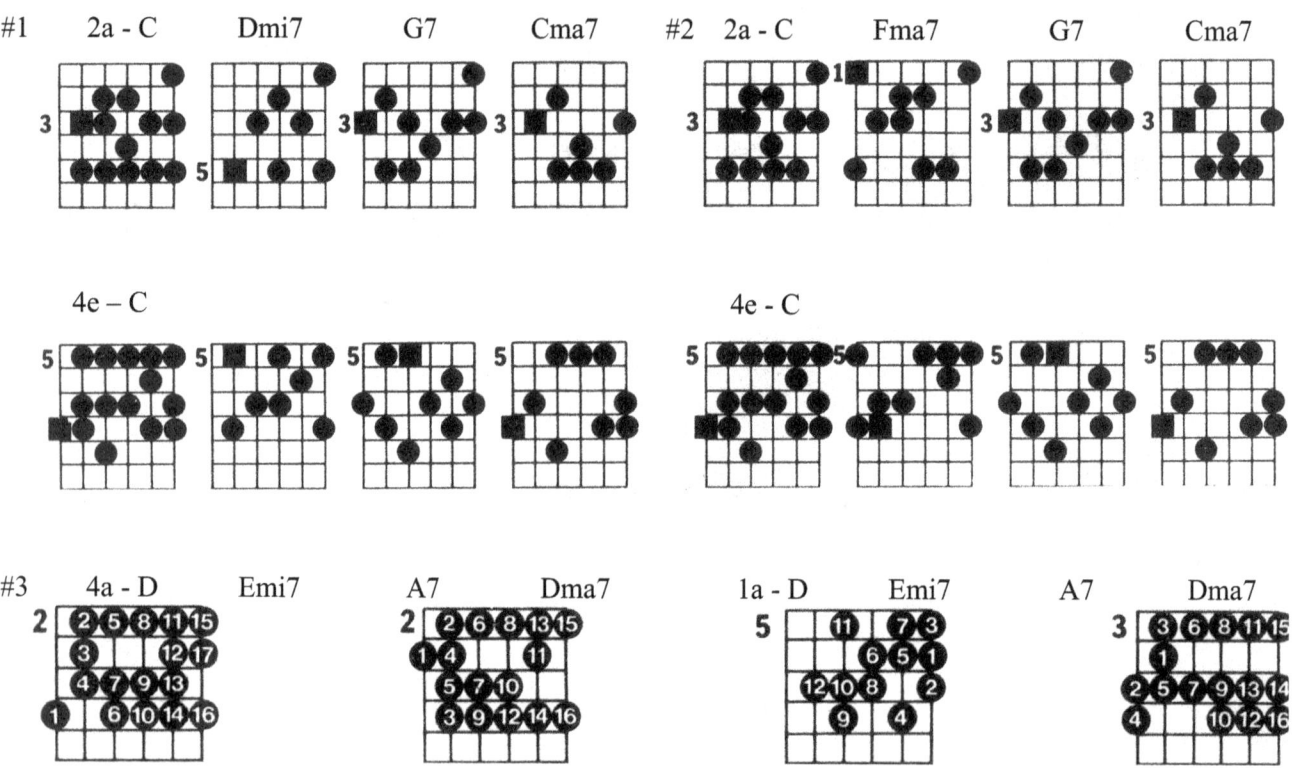

Arpeggio Review Continued

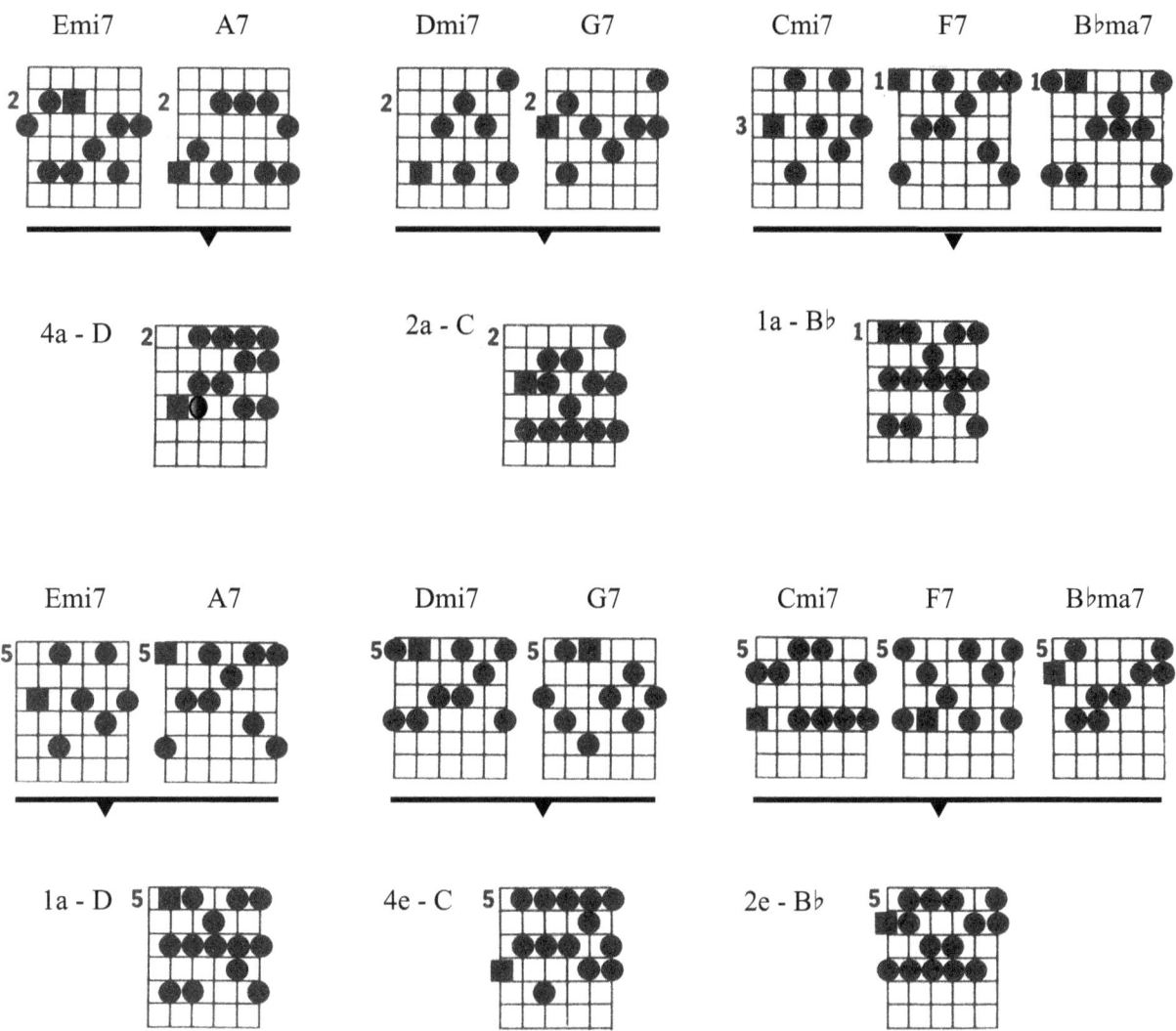

The Sequence: Melodic Patterns Combined With Arpeggios

(This is a bit of an advanced topic, but try it out and if you want to pursue it, you'll know how.-LW)

We've covered melodic patterns earlier in the book, where we used them as exercises to build dexterity and speed in scales. One melodic pattern is even demonstrated from chord tones only. Here's the idea behind sequences:

A sequence is a musical term describing a melodic or harmonic structure that is *repeated from a different note*. Sequences can be the same type of pattern as the original, or even a variation of it as long as you can hear that the second version is related to the first.

To experiment with sequences, take one of the melodic patterns from the earlier lesson, say the one that is spelled C - D - E - C, and using that melodic shape (up two scale tones then back to the first note), try to play it from each note in an arpeggio (or at least the first two or three notes of the arpeggio). This is a terrific way to build melodies while keeping something related to the song, and is an important tool. Jazz players (especially players like guitarist Joe Pass) use this idea extensively. They take the melody of a song and move it around. Beethoven too!

Because jazz changes fly by so quickly, they often outline the chord by playing the sequence from the 3rd and 7th of the chord (E is the 3rd of Cma7, B is the 7th). Doing that with the melodic pattern above, for example, you'd play E - F - G - E and then B - C - D - B. Try it with the chord progressions in this review.

Lesson 21

Arpeggios and Their Diatonic Extensions

The goal of this lesson is to show you the arpeggios you have already seen, with notes from the scale added to them. Notes from the scale added to a chord or arpeggio from the same scale, are called DIATONIC EXTENSIONS. (Diatonic means "of the scale". Extension means "extending the sound".) In the same way that you can change a C major seventh chord into a C major ninth chord, you can change a C major seventh arpeggio into a C major ninth arpeggio.

$$Cma7 = C\ E\ G\ B$$
$$Cma9 = C\ E\ G\ B\ \mathbf{D}$$

In the above example, the D note is a diatonic extension on the Cma7 chord. Adding a diatonic extension note to a chord OR arpeggio looks like a small change on paper. However, the subtle difference in sound is VERY IMPORTANT. That is why we have isolated the diatonic extensions into a separate lesson. These arpeggios are grouped in the same fashion as before.

Diatonic Arpeggios with the 6th Added

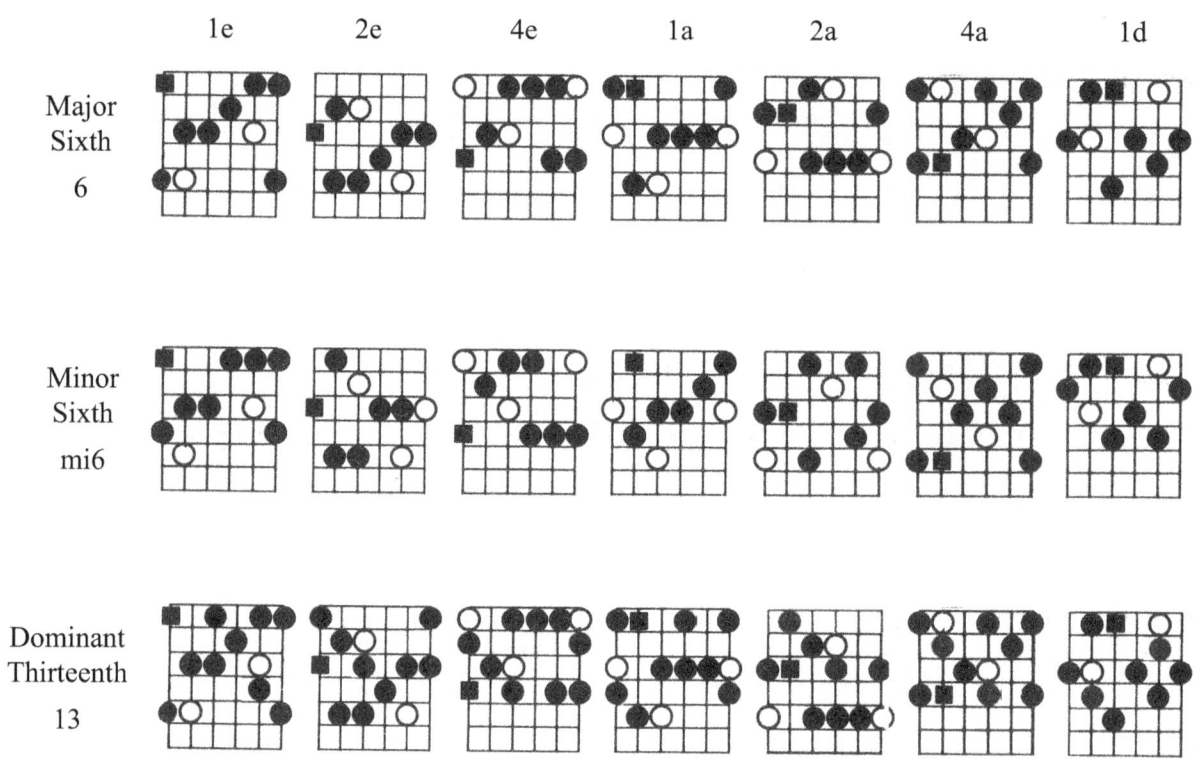

Please Note: The dominant 13th arpeggio shown here has the following notes: Root (R) 3 5 b7 13 (6). The 9th and 11th are omitted. Played as a chord, these notes could receive the alternate name of "7/6" as in "F seven-six."

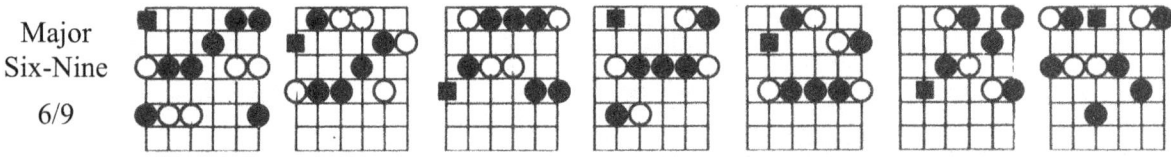

Diatonic Arpeggios with the 9th Included

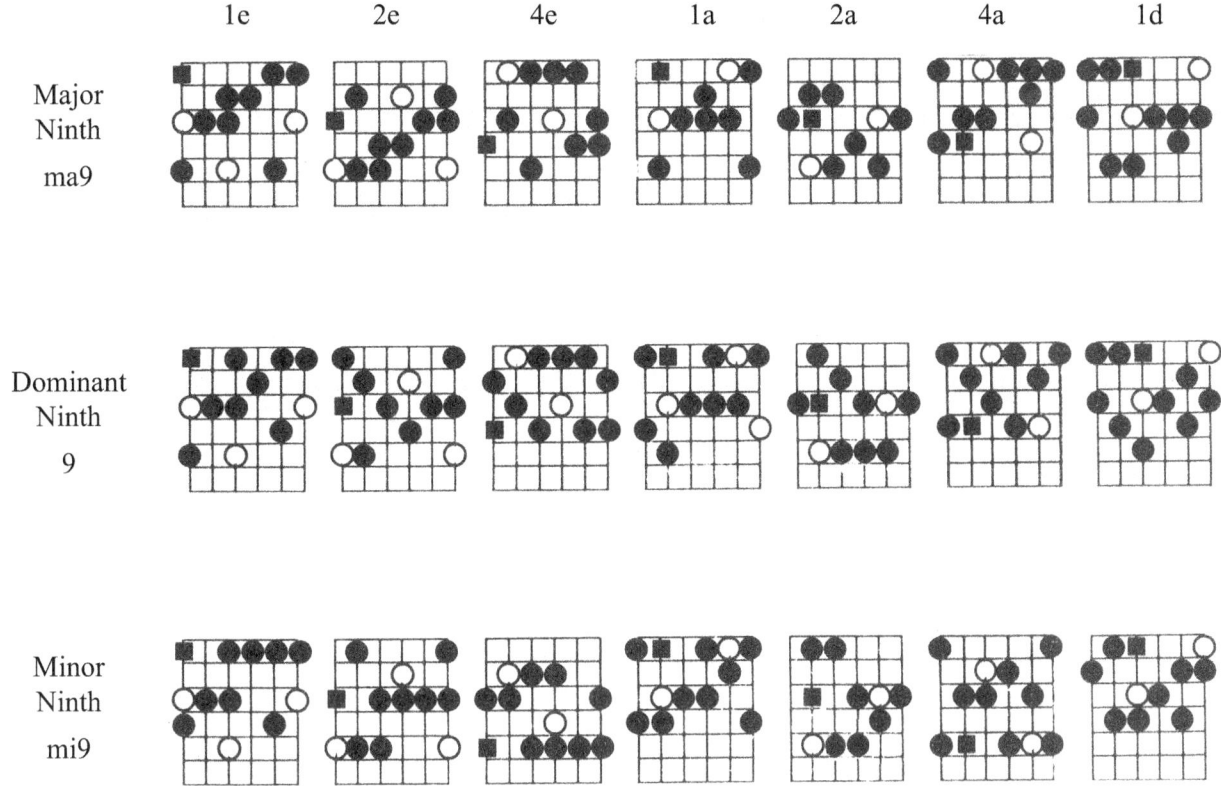

Diatonic Extension on Chords in the Major Scale

Which chords in the major scale include the chords with diatonic extensions? The table below lists the extended chords that occur on each scale degree.

I	ii	iii	IV	V	vi	vii
Cma7	Dmi7	Emi7	Fma7	G7	Ami7	Bmi7♭5
Cma9	Dmi9		Fma9	G9	Ami9	(B dim)
C6/9			F6/9	G6/9		
Cma11	Dmi11	Emi11		G11	Ami11	
Cma13	Dmi13	Emi7#5	Fma13	G11	Ami7#5	Bmi7#5

Lesson 22

The Diminished Seventh Arpeggio

The diminished seventh chord does not occur naturally in the Major diatonic scale. However, it is seen so frequently, we will show you the chord and its arpeggios now, so that you may use them in your playing right away. A diminished seventh chord can be built by lowering the 3, 5, and 7 of a dominant seventh chord.

C E G B♭ = C dominant 7th   C E♭ G♭ B♭♭ (A) = C diminished 7th*

*B♭♭ - This is "B double flat." When you take a note with a flat and flat it again (lower it another 1/2 step), you get a note called a double flat. A coincidence of music is the fact that B♭♭ = A. The same holds true for sharps. (Fx = G. 'x' is the double sharp sign.)

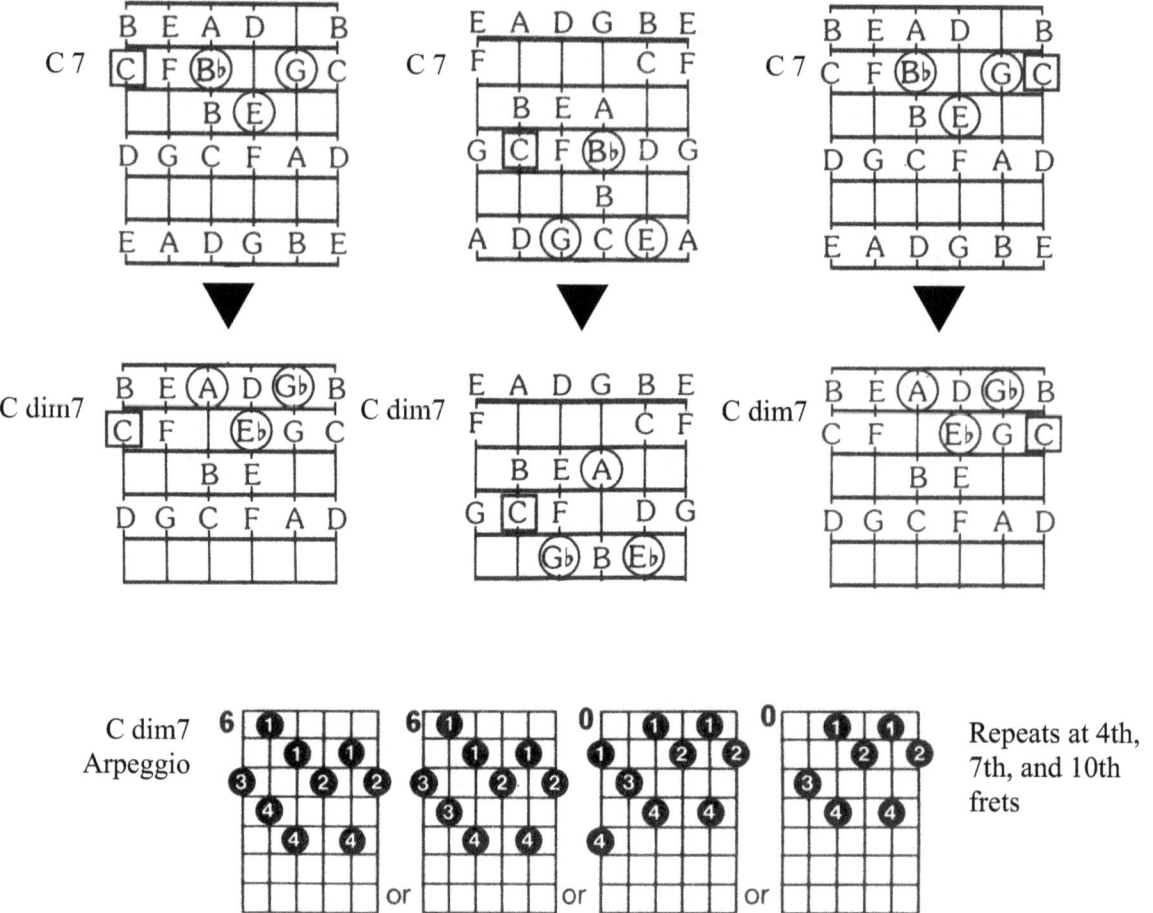

Repeats at 4th, 7th, and 10th frets

My favorite seems to be the last fingering.

Styles for the Studio by Leon White • 40

Diminished Seventh Progression Examples

Play these examples as we have done before. The diminished seventh chord is frequently found in blues ("Keys to the Kingdom" by B.B. King, for example).

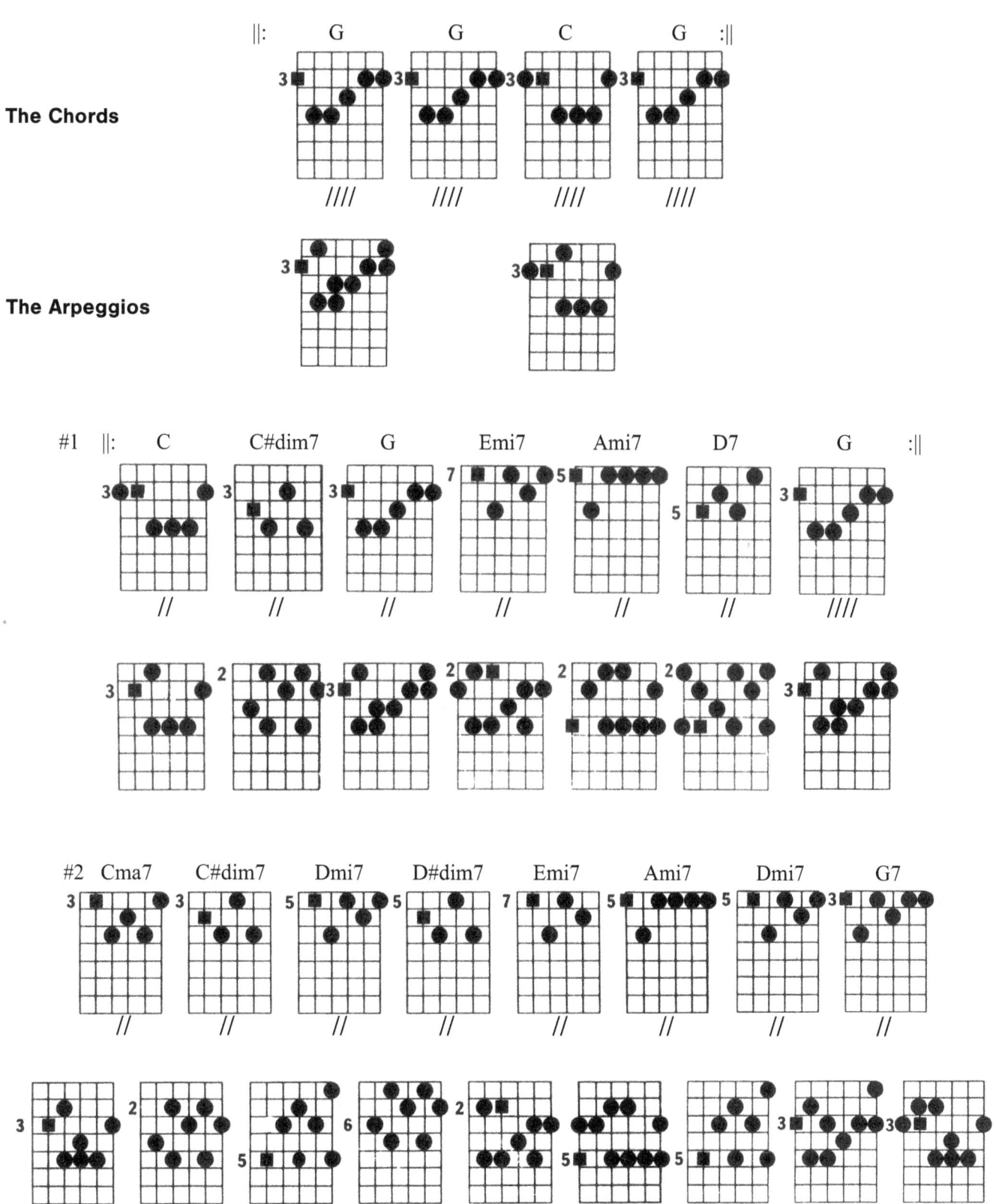

Lesson 23

A Word on Ear Training

From my teaching experience I have found that many players who are learning to improvise for the first time, tend to be very mechanical in their effort. They learn which scales work with which chords, and then all they do is RANDOMLY select notes from the scale, to play. There is nothing wrong with experimentation. (As you must know by now, I encourage it.) However, the purpose of experimentation is to discover new vocabulary words for you to use in improvisation - that is - to find new interval sounds and sequences of intervals.

Once you locate the sounds that appeal to you, you must LEARN THEM - you want to be able to hear them inside your head, so that you can CONSTRUCT a meaningful (at least to you) melodic line. What it all comes down to is this: Good improvising is not randomly collecting or expressing interval sounds. Improvising is playing the music that you hear inside yourself.

A good sentence in language has a beginning, a middle, and an end. The communication takes you from point A to point B. Most popular songs do the same thing, and your solos should also be doing this. A good improviser has INTENT - He has a feeling inside himself which his brain is trying to translate into a melody in his head, and which he then tries to find on his guitar. A less accomplished improviser knows only that a certain group of notes is O.K., so he just selects the notes from this group.

Another pitfall this attitude creates is a dependence on "licks." Licks are "safe" (always acceptable) sounds that are played when we can think of nothing else (or we are afraid to try anything new). They can become a crutch because we know they'll work before we play them. Licks exist for every player - they are the "security blanket" of improvising. Try to become aware of your own licks, and accept them for what they are, a means to help you develop melodies, nothing more.

How can you overcome a dependence on "lick playing?" The answer is twofold. 1) Really learn where sounds are located on the guitar (which is the purpose of this book) and 2) Develop your ability to create melodies. This is where EAR TRAINING comes into play.

What is Ear Training??

Ear training is a MEMORY FUNCTION with which you remember interval sounds. You remember sounds so that your brain may recall them whenever you want to put these sounds together to create a melody (and music in general). You are trying to create a melody to express something.

How Do You Do This?

Your memory is stimulated by REPETITION. Ear training is accomplished by exposing your musical memory to a sound over and over, until you can remember it and recall it from your memory, whenever you want. Whenever you can sing or play anything from memory, you are experiencing the results of ear training. What can you do to help your musical memory?

As you practice your scales and arpeggios from now on, try singing them (or humming them) to yourself as you play. Gradually you will be able to sing them without playing them - that is, from your memory. The net result of all this is that you will be able to make up melodies in your head, and then play them on the guitar. This process will take some time. But the more you do this the better you will become. Guitarist George Benson is known for his scat singing along with his solos (check out his recording of "This Masquerade").

A very important by-product of this effort will be an increase in your ability to recognize musical sounds in the air, as they come to you from other players. Other players in the band won't have to tell you, "Hey, we're playing Blues in C," you'll be able to recognize the chord pattern. You'll hear what they play, and respond by playing something back - TOTAL NON VERBAL COMMUNICATION. Your brain will be 'talking' with their brains, through the language of musical sound - a very exciting, spontaneous, and meaningful way to communicate.

Repetition - so you can hear it "inside your head."

Lesson 24
New Scales

In this lesson we will continue our study of melodic resources, and begin working with scales other than the seven note diatonic major scale we have already seen. The scales that will be covered here are:

The Pentatonic minor scale **The Pentatonic major scale** **The Dorian scale**
The Blues scale **The Mixolydian scale**

These scales can be played over many different chords, frequently in the same progression. You have already seen an example of this when we discussed the use of the major scale with chords in its key. These scales are often used in Rock, Blues, and Country musical styles.

Scales and Modes

Mode: In modern usage, a mode is a group of notes, like a scale, and derived from a scale (most commonly discussed using the major scale). Simply stated, a mode is made by playing a major scale from a note *other than the root*. Doing so creates a different sound to our ears because of the sequence of half step and whole step intervals.

Let's take a quick look:

C Major Scale	C	D	E	F	G	A	B	C		
Dorian Mode		D	E	F	G	A	B	C	D	
Phrygian Mode			E	F	G	A	B	C	D	E
Lydian Mode				F	G	A	B	C	D	E	F
Mixolydian					G	A	B	C	D	E	F	G
Aeolian Mode						A	B	C	D	E	F	G	A
Locrian Mode							B	C	D	E	F	G	A	B

The modes are built to be one octave in length (like a major scale), so they each contain seven notes. The variation in sound comes from our musical brain hearing the first note as the 'root' of the sound. Not all of the basic modes are commonly heard in modern music, mostly because of their sound.

The key element is that modes sound different, but are just as valid as a major scale when it comes to improvising or composing. The emphasis on the mode being *derived* from another scale can be a distraction in understanding intervals and sounds when first improvising. For that reason, and to re-inforce hearing intervals from the root tonality and location, I'm making a break (or brake) with tradition and referring to the Dorian and Mixolydian tone groups as scales. This has the additional benefits of being consistent with the Pentatonic scales and arpeggios discussed, and preparing you for jazz improvising. Of the modes above, we'll focus only on the Dorian and Mixolydian "scales."

Study one scale at a time, carefully. This section has a lot of material, so don't race through it; there are many applications for everything. (You've read that before somewhere, haven't you? "Ah, yes, Virginia, you have," her father murmured before passing the salad and a kidney stone.)

You may not be able to use all the fingerings shown for each scale immediately, but try to learn at least three fingerings for each scale; transfer the six melodic patterns you know to each of these new scales. Progressions with suggested chord voicings are shown; practice the progressions with another guitarist or a backing track if you can. If you are playing alone, strum the chord once, and then play your "line" afterward. Repeat this for each chord in the progression.

Our examples will show basic chords to support each scale. Remember, the scales can be used wherever you think they sound good. The purpose of the examples is to give you a starting point, and a place to practice *hearing the scales*. We cannot emphasize how important it is to explore and experiment with new material.

Below is a brief outline of how to learn and use new scales:

1. Memorize the new fingering(s).
2. Get used to the new sound (this will take a little time - usually about as long as it takes to learn the fingerings.)
3. Learn where the scale can be used; that is, with what chords (we'll be showing you some).
4. Play the scale to develop speed and confidence with it. Use the melodic patterns for this.
5. Play the scale with chords, and then with chord progressions. Each new scale has several fingerings.

We recommend memorizing the fingerings for each scale, as a group. It's good for both your right hand and left hand technique, and it will increase your familiarity with ALL parts of the fingerboard. As you memorize the fingerings, and "fool around" with them, little riffs and melodies will occur to you from different parts of different fingerings. Move these riffs to all of the other fingerings for that scale. If you do this, you will improve your ear and your ability to improvise in different locations on the guitar. You will be extending your power and confidence to all parts of the guitar - not just your "favorite" spots.

How to Play these Scales with Chord Progressions

1. Play the chord progression as shown until you are familiar with it. Really try to make it sound good; make it bluesy or whatever style you like.

If you're working alone:

2. Play the first chord of the progression with one strum. Then play the scale, ascending and descending slowly. Then play the next chord and do the same thing again. This helps you to hear the progression and scale sounds together.
3. Once you are comfortable with the scale ascending and descending, repeat Step #2 above, but play the melodic patterns you know, instead of the scale. Remember, take your time - if you rush here, you'll never understand the more advanced scales.

With backing tracks or another guitarist:

4. Play the progression slowly while you play the scale. Play the scale SLOWLY at first. When you are comfortable with the scale fingering, try the melodic patterns over the progression, as we did above.

WARNING: The more impatient you are here, the worse you'll play. Play everything slowly, smoothly and under control. There is nothing wrong with fast playing, but first comes slow playing.

Lesson 25

The Minor Pentatonic Scale

The Pentatonic scales are five note scales. We are going to discuss two of the most popular ones. The first scale is a very "Bluesy" sounding scale, while the second is a major, "sweet-country" sound.

You will probably discover the 1e/1a and 4e/4a fingerings are the most natural fingerings to use with this scale, as you first learn it. However, please remember that the convenience of one fingering in the beginning should not blind you to the other fingerings. BECOME FAMILIAR WITH THEM ALL - you'll know your guitar better, and you'll never be "out of position" (somewhere on the fingerboard where you can't find the right notes to play).

The Major Scale	C	D	E	F	G	A	B	C
The Minor Pentatonic Scale	C	Eb		F	G		Bb	C
	1	b3		4	5		b7	

As you can see, of the notes present in the minor pentatonic, the b3 and the b7, are *not found* in the Major scale. Since the Minor Pentatonic scale has dropped the 2nd and 6th notes (D and A in the key of C major), the b3 and b7 stand out more when heard.

As before, we are going to study the fingerings in two groups. The first group is easier, the second more difficult.

Practice the scales slowly and carefully. Use alternate picking, and review our fingering rules in the major scale lesson if you become confused with the fingerings.

Learn the fingerings and then try the scale with the progressions that follow. The fingerings should feel familiar as they overlap the minor seventh arpeggio fingerings you already know.

Group One

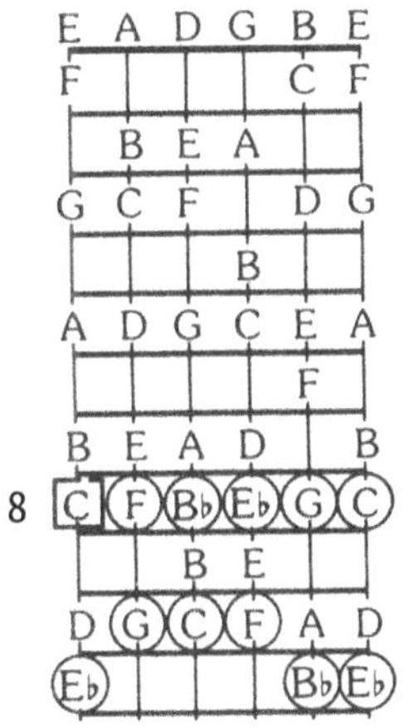

1e — Root C   4e — Root C   1a — Root C   4a — Root F

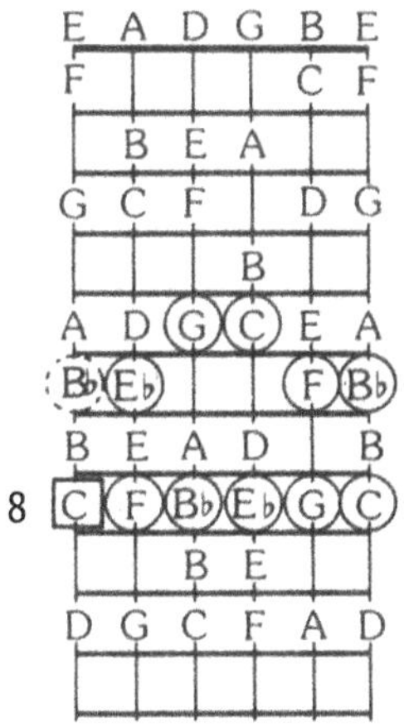

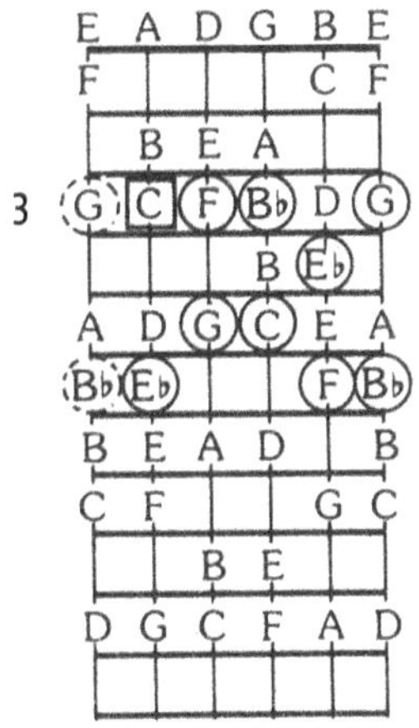

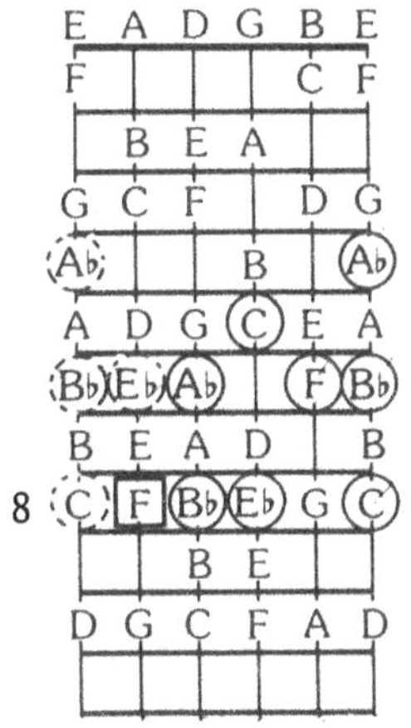

Group Two

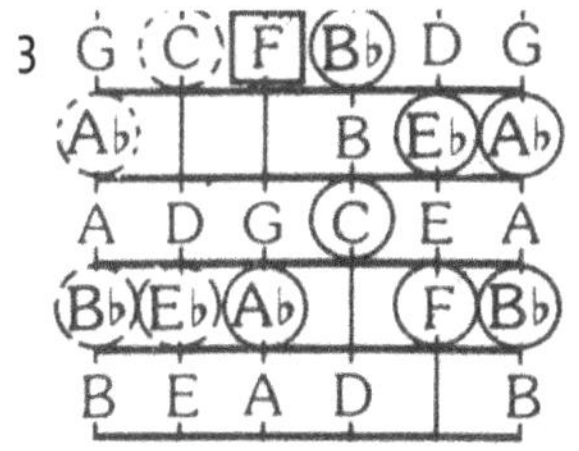

1d — Root F   3e — Root C   3a — Root C

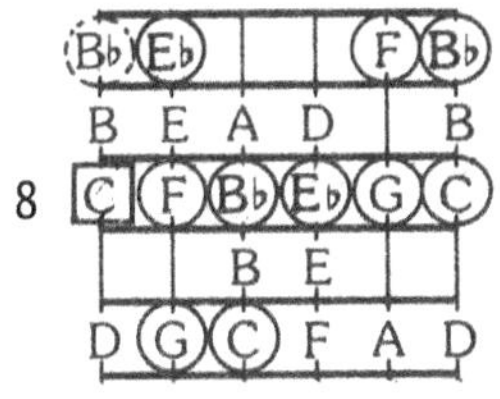

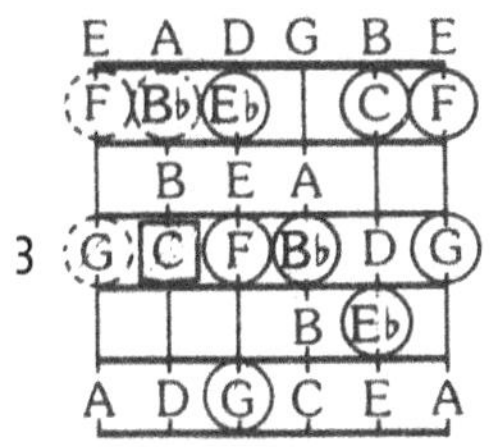

Styles for the Studio by Leon White

Sample Progressions for the C Minor Pentatonic Scale

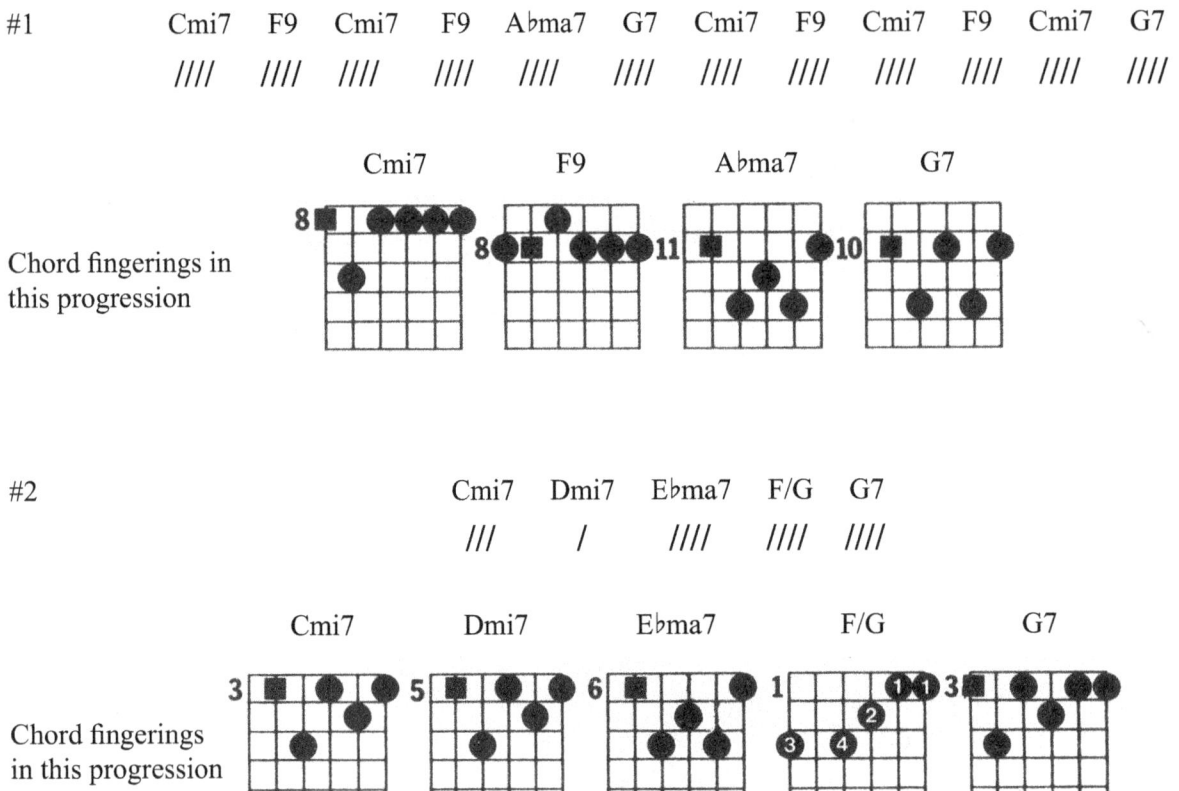

The 3e and 3a Fingerings

I will be the first to admit these are awkward fingerings at first. If you take the minor pentatonics from the root C and look for the B♭ major scale in the same location, they will seem less odd. For the fingering from the root F look for an E♭ major scale fingering in that location. I'll remind you again that all this stuff *does* fit together if you just let it.

Lesson 26

The Major Pentatonic Scale

C	D	E	F	G	A	B	C	C Major Scale
C	**D**	**E**		**G**	**A**		**C**	C Major Pentatonic Scale
1	2(9)	3		5	6(13)			

This scale places emphasis on the 6th and 9th sounds. Because there is no seventh in it, you can play it with dominant chords (that have the ♭7) *or* Major chords (that have the ♮7 in them). The 6/9 sound can also be emphasized here and is traditionally a "sweet-country" kind of sound, as shown in Example #1. You'll also find these sounds in many fills on Motown recordings, and from players like Steve Cropper.

Like the minor pentatonic scale, the major pentatonic scale is similar to arpeggios found in the major scale fingerings.

Also note that the minor pentatonic and major pentatonic fingerings contain the same notes. (Yes, I said the same!) They just start from a different note as a root. Compare the 4e Root C major pentatonic with 1e A minor pentatonic. ("These pesky fingerings! Are they all the same?" Sometimes it seems like it.)

Just one note or interval can make a huge difference. That's why I'm showing you the sounds a little bit at a time. It is all about the musical sound and melody.

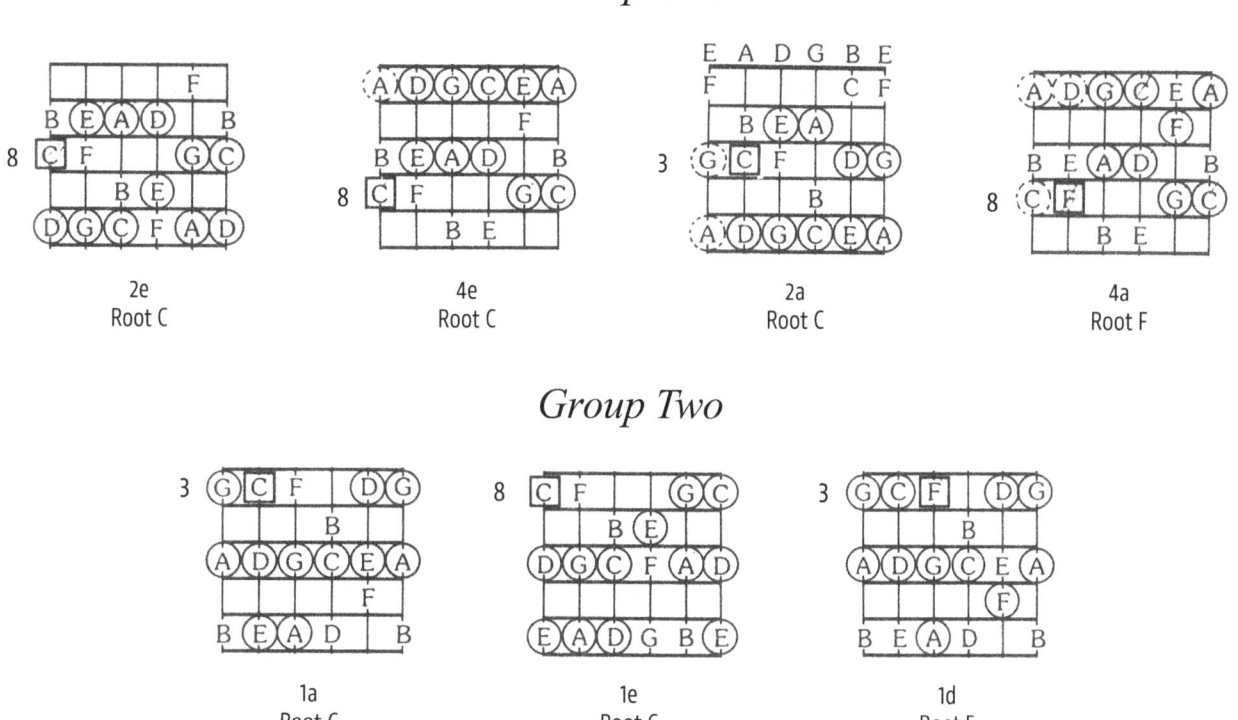

Compare these fingerings to those of the ordinary C Major scale. Can you see that all of the fingerings overlap? *In fact the major pentatonic scale could also be thought of as selected notes of the major scale...* (There will be more on this in the Scale Review.) If you're looking for a C6/9 arpeggio, you've found it.

This should simplify your memorization of these fingerings. Play the C Major scale fingering 2e, and the C Major Pentatonic scale 2e. The Major Pentatonic is just emphasizing selected notes of the Major Scale. Following are shown the Major Pentatonic fingerings, with the scale tones of the *major scale*, in black.

Group One with Major Scale Tones Added

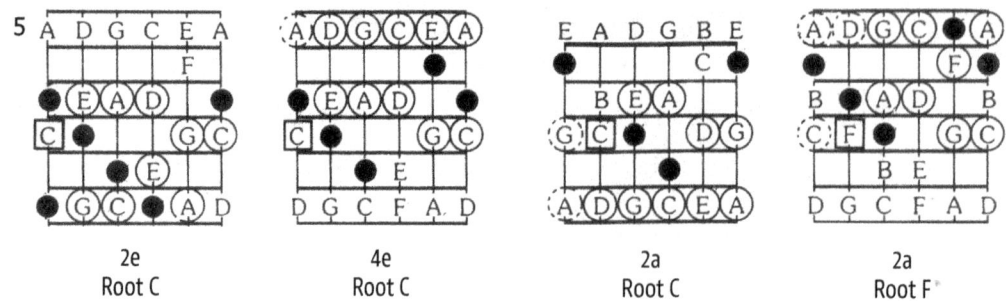

Group Two with Major Scale Tones Added

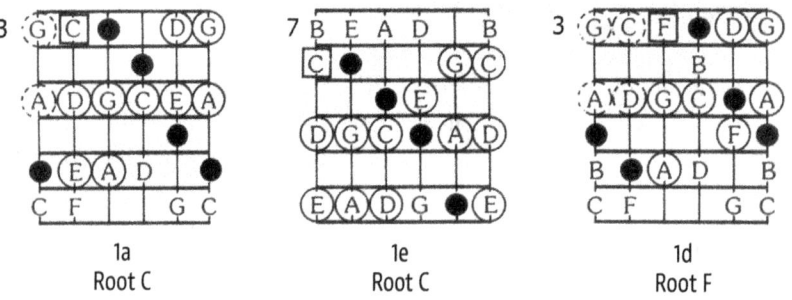

Below are some sample melodies built from the various Major Pentatonic fingerings. As we have done before, locate the fingering, play the scale a couple of times to help remember it, and then play the melody line.

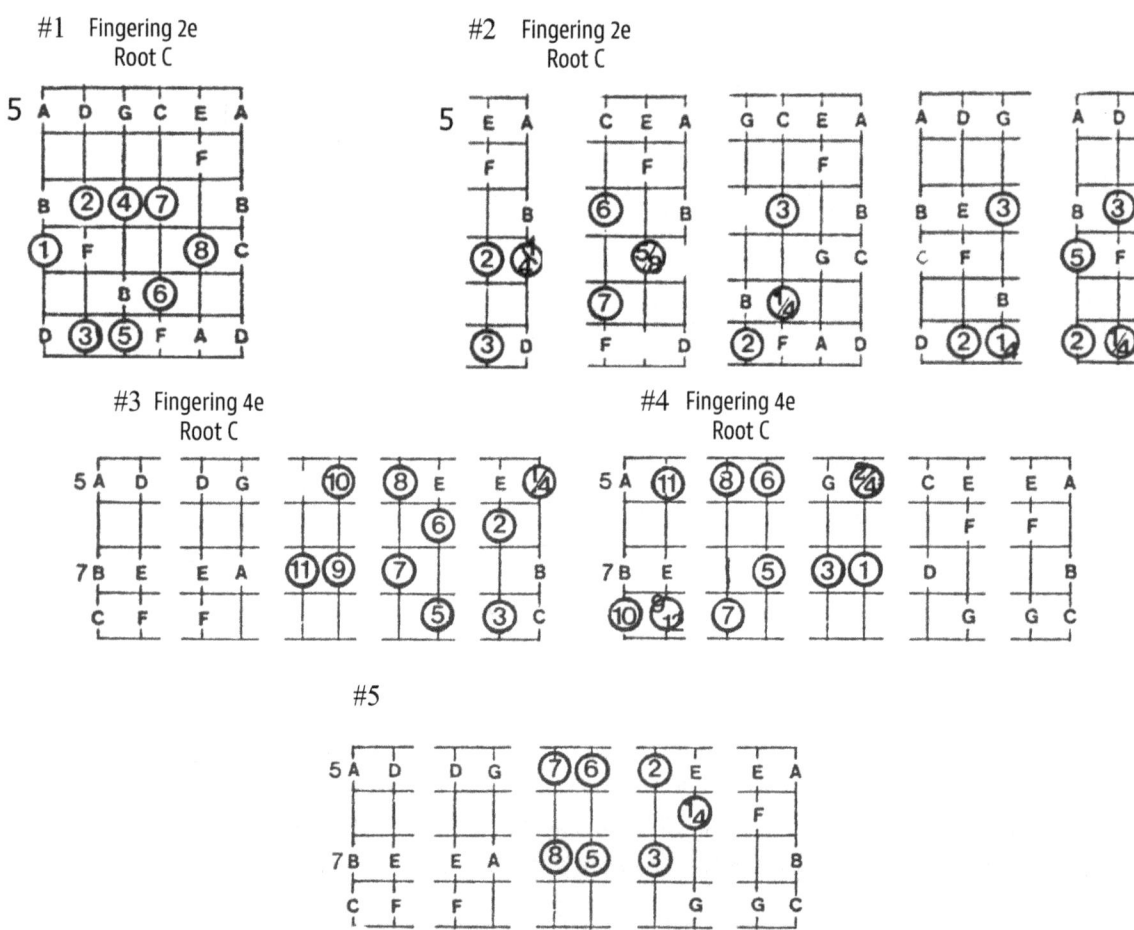

Lesson 27

The Dorian Scale

The Dorian scale is the first of our new 7 note scales. It can be played over several chords or a whole progression in the same way as the Pentatonic scales. The Dorian sound lends itself to the 'Blues-Jazz Rock' type of playing. (Note the similarity between this scale and the minor pentatonic scale.)

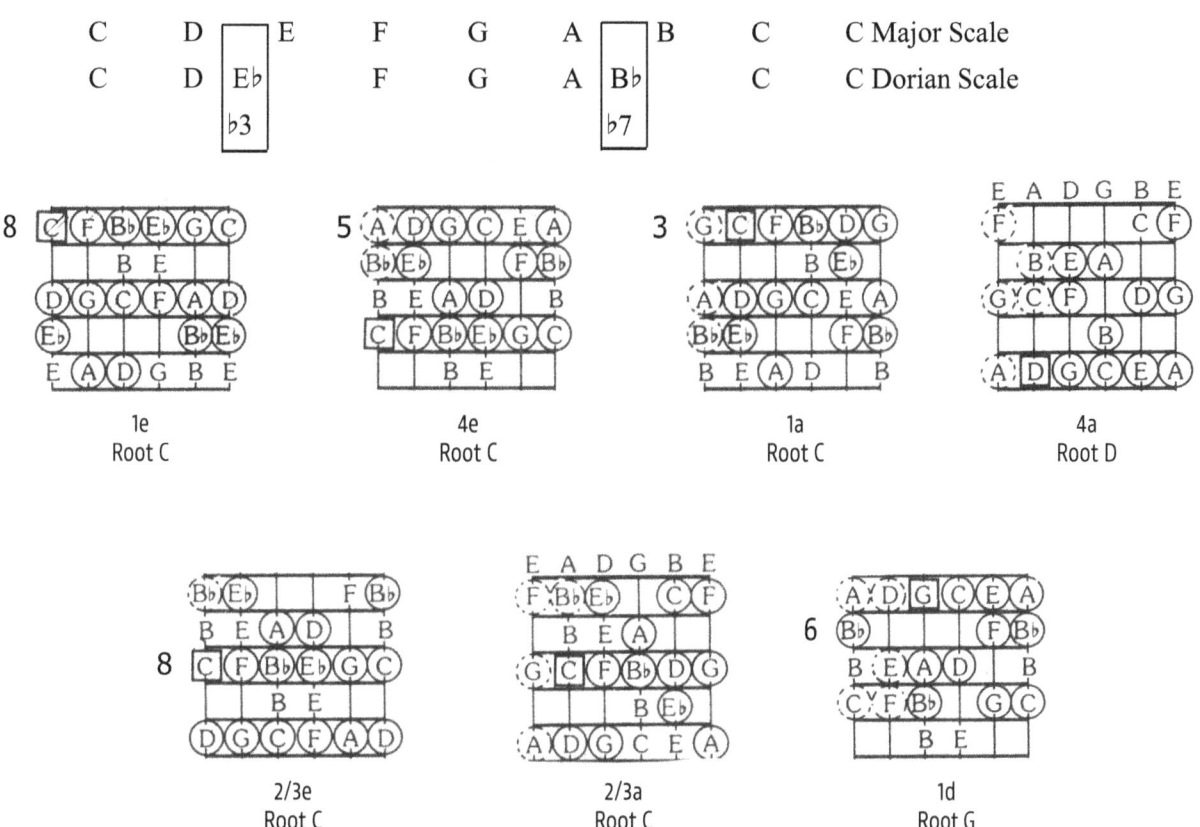

Sample Chord Progressions

Try the Dorian scale in the progressions where you have used the Minor Pentatonic.

Play the C Dorian for all of these progressions.

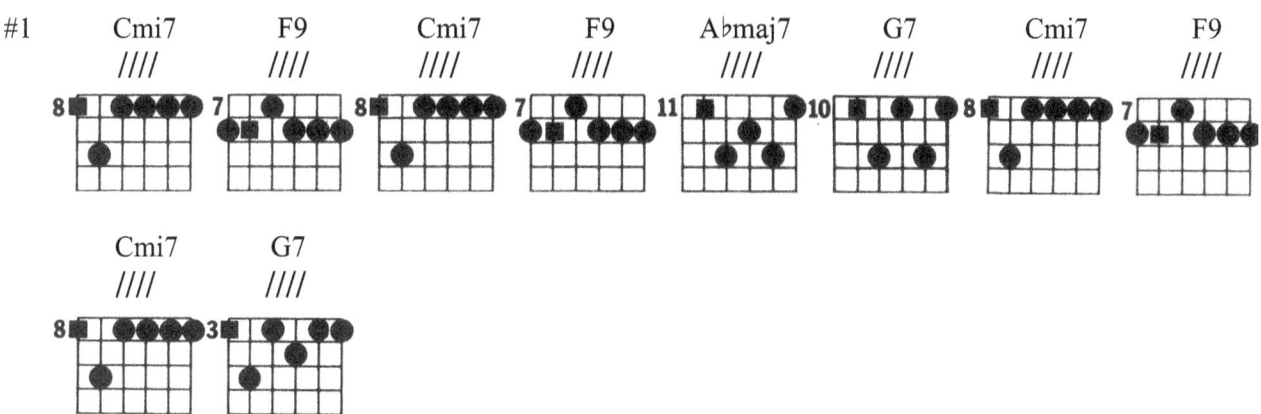

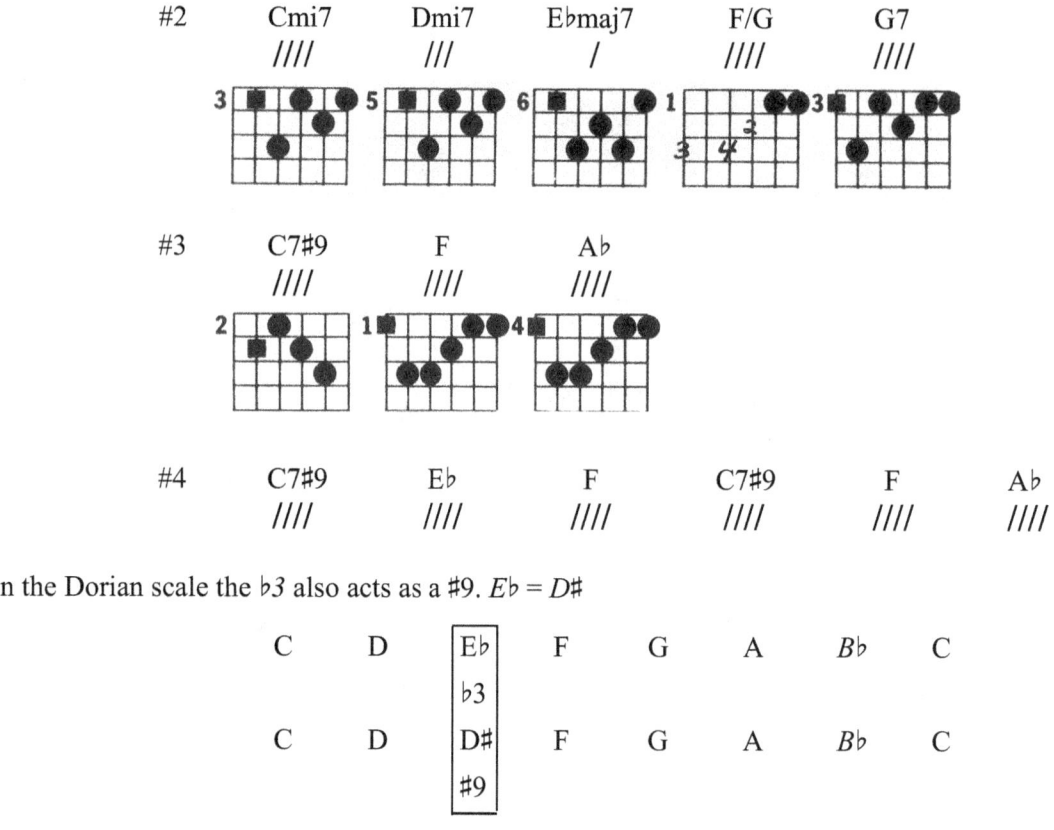

In the Dorian scale the ♭3 also acts as a #9. E♭ = D#

C	D	E♭	F	G	A	B♭	C
		♭3					
C	D	D#	F	G	A	B♭	C
		#9					

Compare the Dorian and Minor Pentatonic fingerings (as shown below). Can you see that the minor pentatonic scale fingerings are contained inside the Dorian, the same way as the Major Pentatonic was contained in the Major scale?

Play the C Dorian 1e and then the C Minor Pentatonic 1e. As before, the Minor Pentatonic is emphasizing notes of the Dorian. Since the fingerings do overlap, your memorization time should be cut in half. The two scales should **reinforce** each other's sounds and fingerings, not compete or confuse. Review both scales thoroughly if this is not clear. Shown below are **Dorian** fingerings, with the corresponding minor pentatonic notes shown in black.

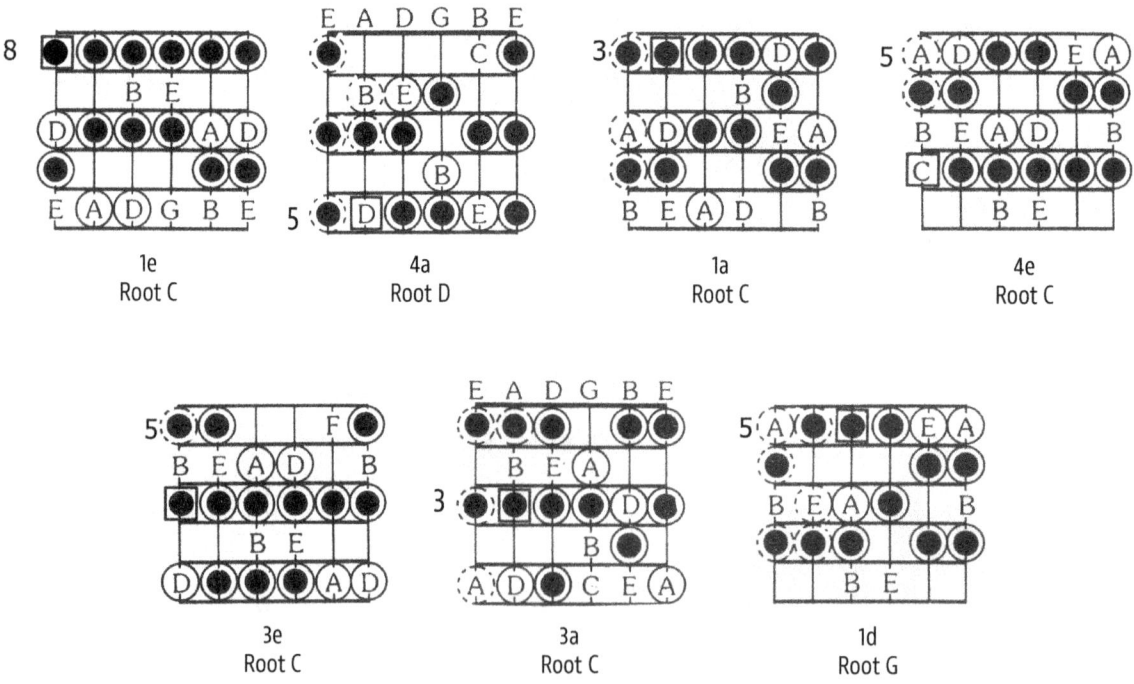

Here are some sample "solos" from the Dorian Scale. 1-5 may be played over a C or Cmi7 chord; #6 over a G or Gmi7 chord.

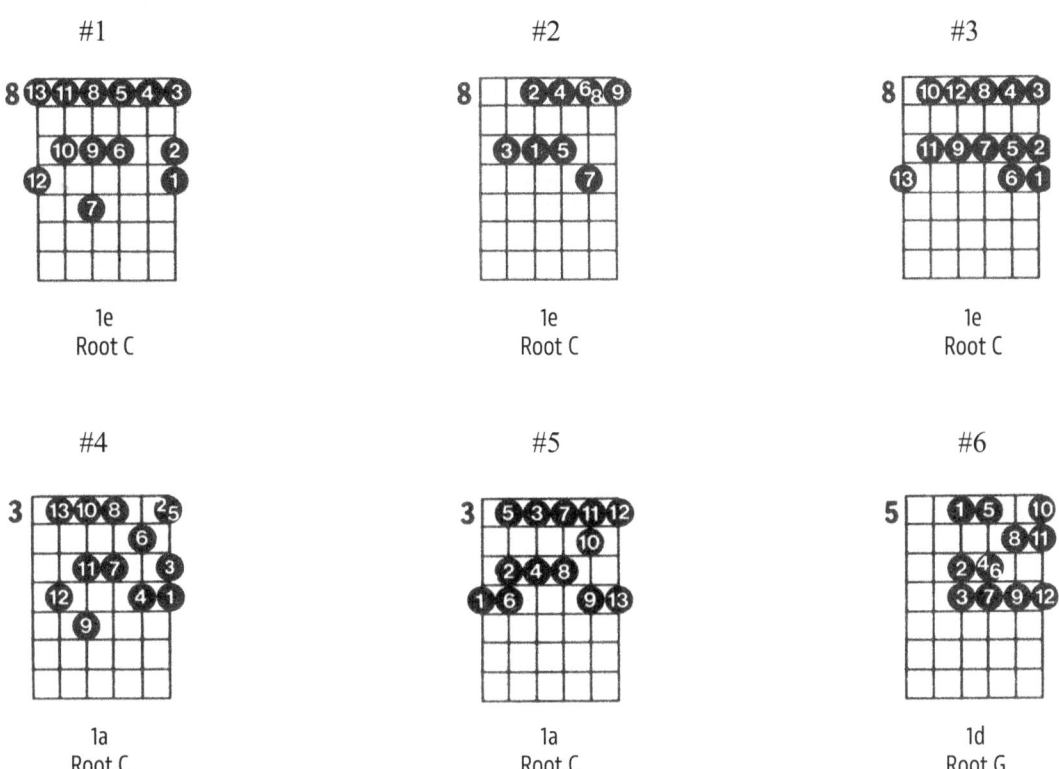

Lesson 28

The Blues Scale

C	D	E	F		G	A	B	C	**C Major Scale**
C	Eb		F	F#	G		Bb	C	C Blues Scale
1	b3		4	#4	5		b7		

The blues scale is our first *altered scale*. It has six notes (plus the octave), and there are three notes in a row that are only a half-step apart (F, F#, and G). In addition, we have a scale that has *two notes with the same alphabetic letter* in their names (F and F#). Below is a comparison of the blues scale and other scales you have already seen:

C Major Scale	C	D	E	F		G	A	B	C
C Dorian Scale	C	D Eb		F		G	A Bb		C
C Minor Pentatonic	C		Eb	F		G		Bb	C
C Blues Scale	C		Eb	F	F#	G		Bb	C

Because of the unusual construction of this scale, several of the fingerings may be played in more than one way; there are also some unusual stretches.

Group One

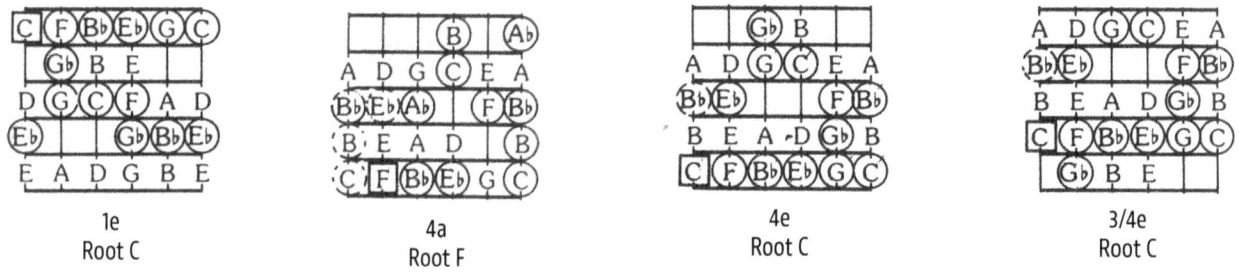

1e
Root C

4a
Root F

4e
Root C

3/4e
Root C

Group Two

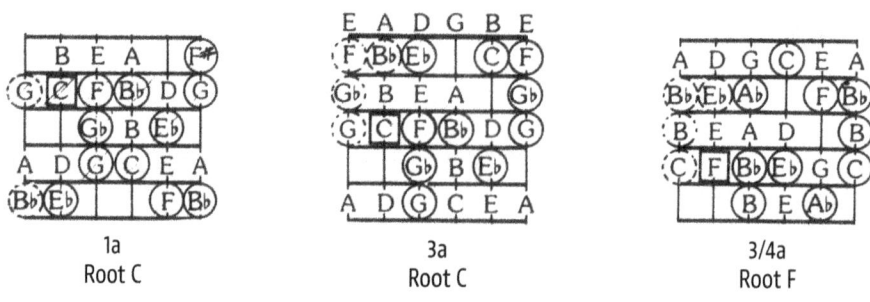

1a
Root C

3a
Root C

3/4a
Root F

Compare the Blues Scale to the minor pentatonic scale. Can you see that the Blues scale is the minor pentatonic with a ♯4 note added? As before, the importance of the Blues scale is that it is calling your attention to this new note - the ♯4 (F♯ in the scale of C).

Play a C minor pentatonic and a C Blues scale in the same position. Can you see that the fingerings overlap and interlock? (See, I *told* you - way back in the major scale introduction . . .)

We have already seen how the Dorian and Minor Pentatonic scales overlap. Can we combine the Dorian, Blues, and minor pentatonic into one group of sounds?

Yes. All of these sounds (shown in the center Diagram below) can be combined, and do work well together.

Return to the Dorian scale fingerings, and look for ♯4 notes that may be located in each fingering. (Remember ... F♯ is the ♯4 of C, G♯ is the ♯4 of D, and C♯ is the ♯4 of G).

The black dots below represent the ♯4 note added to two minor pentatonic fingerings, and one Dorian.

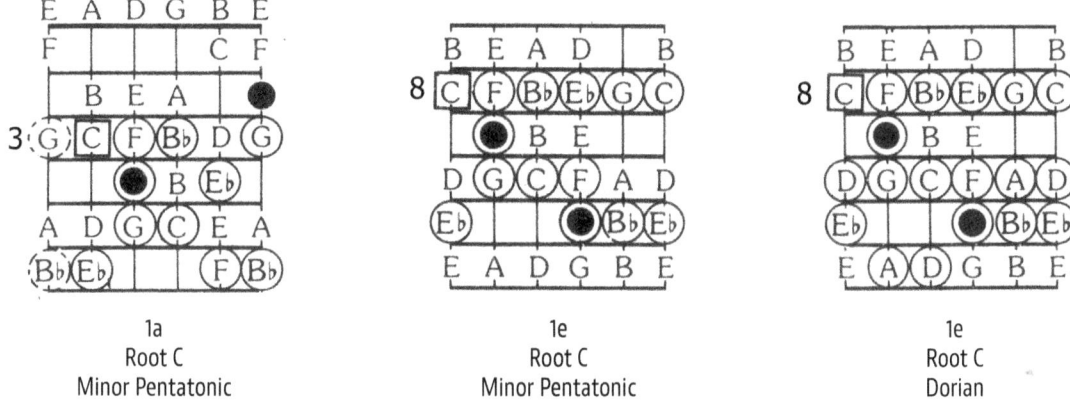

Shown below are some sample "licks" that may be made from the Blues Scale.

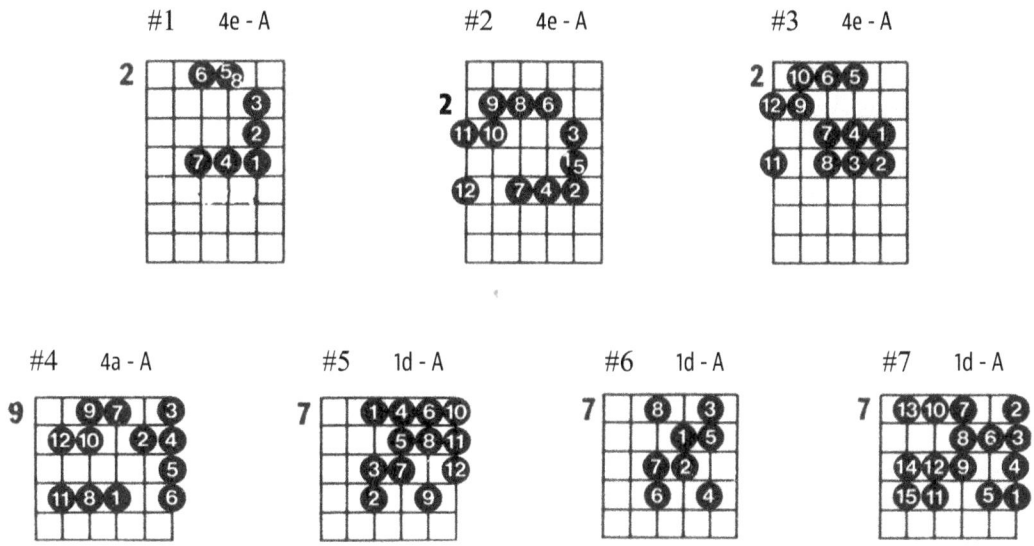

Lesson 29

The Mixolydian Scale

The Mixolydian scale is shown below. The primary difference between it and the Major scale is the lowered 7th degree. This sound tends to imply further movement to some other chord. This scale's basic use is with the V7 chords in any major key. You can try it with almost any dominant seventh chord on any other scale degrees.

C	D	E	F	G	A	B	C	C Major Scale
C	D	E	F	G	A	B♭ ♭7	C	C Mixolydian Scale

The Mixolydian sounds really revolve around the ♮3 and the ♭7 notes used together. This pair of notes really help define the blues sounds, and country-blues sounds. As you look at each fingering below mark the two notes. They have an interesting relationship to each other. (Go ahead . . . E and B♭ from the root C, B and F from the root G.)

The Mixolydian sounds can be used to illustrate an additional approach to applying scales. You can play it over a progression of chords (as we have done with the other scales we have seen so far) and you can also use it with only one chord at a time (that is, every time the chord changes you may move to a new Mixolydian scale).

C7	F7	G7	C7
I	(IV)	V	I

In the progression above you'd think you could play the C Mixolydian scale over the whole thing - but the F7 chord is spelled F A C E♭, while a C Mixolydian scale has an E♮ in it.

The F Mixolydian scale, however, does have that important E♭ in it, so it sounds much better.

In the progression above, one good set of sounds you could use would be as follows:

C7	F7	G7
C Mix.	F Mix.	C Mix. (or G Mix)

(You could play the C Mixolydian scale over the G7 because G7 is the V chord in the Key of C.)

Group One

I'm not going to hide it. You've had these fingerings under your hands as major scale fingerings. C-1e Mixolydian is also the F-1a major scale fingering. (If you recall in our brief discussion of modes we discussed that a mode was a scale started from a note other than the root. Here's an example of it.) B♭-1d Mixolydian is the C-1e major scale.

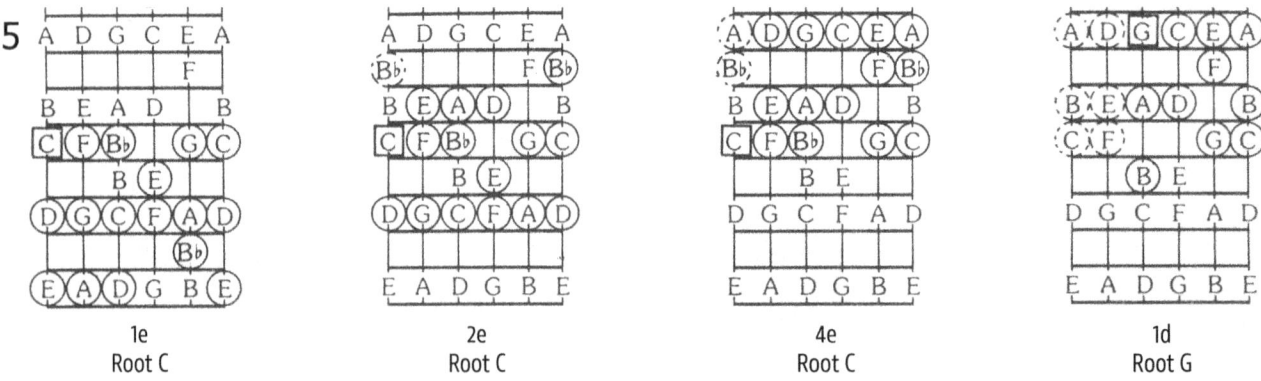

1e Root C   2e Root C   4e Root C   1d Root G

Group Two

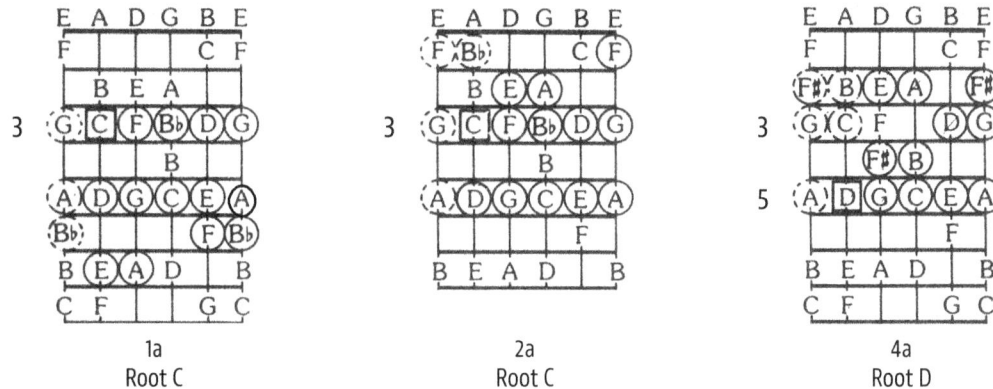

Mixolydian Chord Progression Examples

Play the notes in each box in the order they are numbered. Play the notes smoothly and evenly at first, then make up your own "feel" to this little solo. Each melody for each chord is made up from notes in each of the four Mixolydian scales, placing emphasis on the notes that are emphasized in the Mixolydian sounds (♮3 and ♭7).

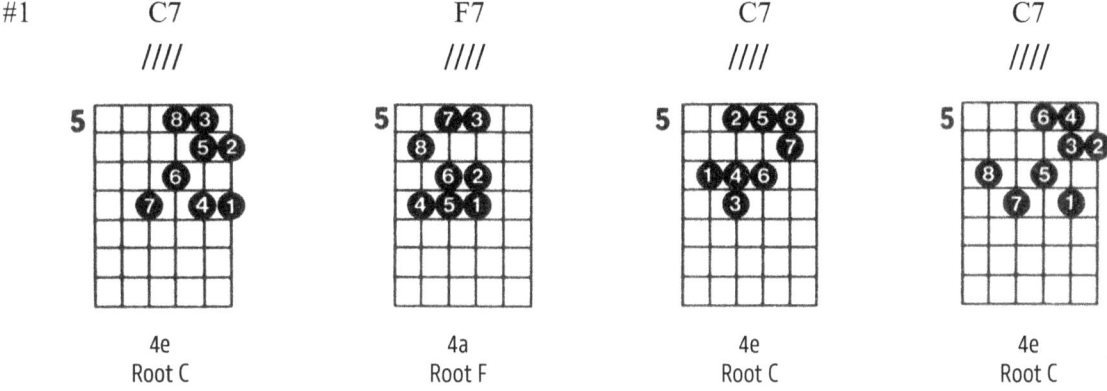

Please note that your left hand does NOT move from the location on the 5th fret in example #1

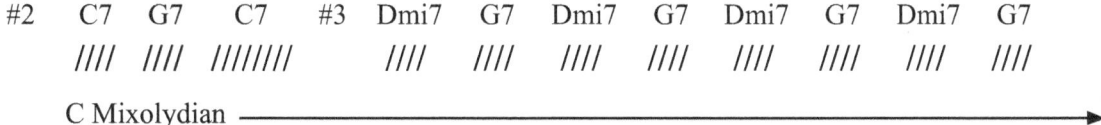

Try the C Mixolydian sounds over a backing track of the progressions in examples #2 and #3.

Lesson 30

In this lesson we are going to review the topics we have covered so far, and discuss the application of scales and arpeggios in more detail.

Review Part A

1. There are two sources of interval sounds in our study of improvisation - the scale and the arpeggio.

2. Scales, in general, contain small interval sounds, while arpeggios contain larger interval sounds.

3. The major scale is the foundation of a large portion of music we enjoy today, and in this study, we have compared all other scales to this major scale.

4. The following scales may be used over entire progressions of chords - the Major scale; the Minor Pentatonic scale; the Major Pentatonic scale; the Dorian scale; the Blues scale.

5. With the Mixolydian scale we introduced the idea that a scale can be used with certain progressions, or it may be used with *one chord at a time.*

6. Arpeggios - Arpeggios are chords played one note at a time, but more importantly, they are large intervals made up from notes in the scale.

7. Arpeggios, because they are chords played one note at a time, generally get applied to one chord at a time.

8. Arpeggios are flexible in terms of the notes they may contain. They may have just the notes of the diatonic chords, (all of them or only a few) and they may contain other notes from the scale in which they belong. These added notes are called *diatonic extensions* (We saw 9ths, 13ths, etc.). Notes out of the scale are referred to "altered tones" or "alterations."

Stacking Arpeggios - A New Idea

Arpeggios may be thought of as chords played one note at a time, or, they may be thought of as *selected notes of the scale.* If you think of them as selected notes of the scale, you have a new application of the arpeggio, for if you can apply any of the notes in a scale to any chord in the scale, then arpeggios (because they are notes of the scale) may be applied to *any chord in the scale too!!* (Well, almost any - the choice is yours.)

Chord   **Arpeggio**

Cma7   C E G B + D F A C = C E G B D F A   **C Major 13th**
                        (Dmi7)   1 3 5 ♮7 9 11 13

                              + E G B D = C E G B D   **C Major 9th**
                       (Emi7)   1 3 5 ♮7 9

C7   C E G B♭ + D F♯ A C = C E G B♭ D F♯ A   **C13♯11** (This example involves 2 keys)
                            (D7)   1 3 5 ♭7 9 ♯11 13

Which arpeggios will work "over" which chords? Given a Cma7 chord (C E G B), arpeggios whose roots are *contained within the original chord,* can frequently be "added" to the chord sound. In this example, DIATONIC chords/arpeggios whose roots are E, G, or B might be tried. (Emi7, G7 or Bmi7♭5 - These are the diatonic arpeggios in the key of C.) Your EAR must evaluate which sounds you prefer, but this is a good starting point . . .

This idea is intended to open you up to an area sometimes referred to as chord stacking, or super imposing chords. (Like when one chord comes over to dinner and never goes home. That is a super imposition.) Many fusion players apply these sounds to create new sounds. It is beyond the scope of this book, but tinker with the idea.

Review Part B

"Do we have only one Giant Scale that contains all of the sounds?" Yes and No. "Yes," we do have one giant group of sounds - our complete set of twelve tones in the chromatic scale (See the reference). "No," in that you should not be trying to play all notes, all the time. Everything will sound the same. Compare the Mixolydian scale to the Dorian scale. There is only one note difference (the ♭3 and ♮3). Yet these two scales *do* sound different.

You *must* be selective. That is why we have introduced the scales one at a time - to show you the effect of individual notes, and restricted (selected) groups of notes. As you play these notes more often, and become better acquainted with them, you will make choices of which sounds you prefer to use in certain instances. Your taste will develop, and your personal preferences will help create your own unique "style" - music that is you. To achieve this, simply continue to play and experiment with the scales, and think about what you like, and what you don't.

Below are sample melodies that show the ♭3 to ♮3 sound. Each box contains one melody. This movement of ♭3 to ♮3 tends to imply a "Bluesey" feel in most instances.

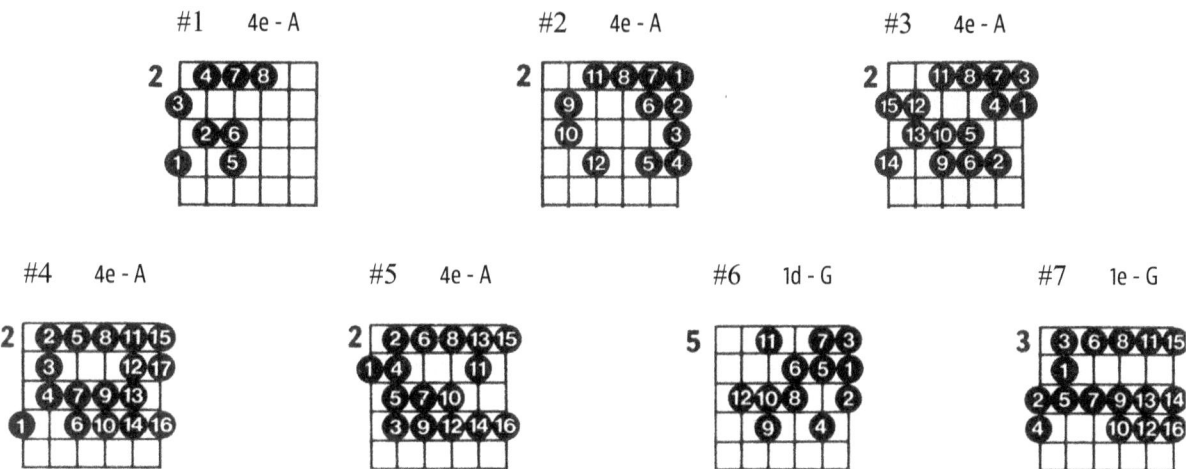

You may play these "licks" over Blues or Blues Rock progressions in the Key of the Root of the example. For instance . . .

4e - A - Play over an A blues progression

1e - G - Play over a G blues progression.

Most of the progressions shown with the Dorian, Blues, and Mixolydian scales, may be used here.

Review Part C - Mixing Scales and Arpeggios

Shown below are several progression examples. In each example we have shown some possibilities for scale and arpeggio application. Remember scales can often be used over an entire progression, while arpeggios can be used with their chords.

Solos: #1 ‖: Gma7   Ami7   D7   Gma7   :‖
              ////   ////   ////   ////

Use: (1) G Maj Scale ──────────────────────────▶

(2) Gma7 (arp.)   Ami7 (arp.)   D7 (arp.)   Gma7 (arp.)

(3) G Maj Scale   Ami7 (arp.)   G Maj Scale   Gma7 (arp.)

(or any combination of scale and arpeggios)

#2 ||: **G**   **G**   **C**   **D**   :||
    ////   ////   ////   ////

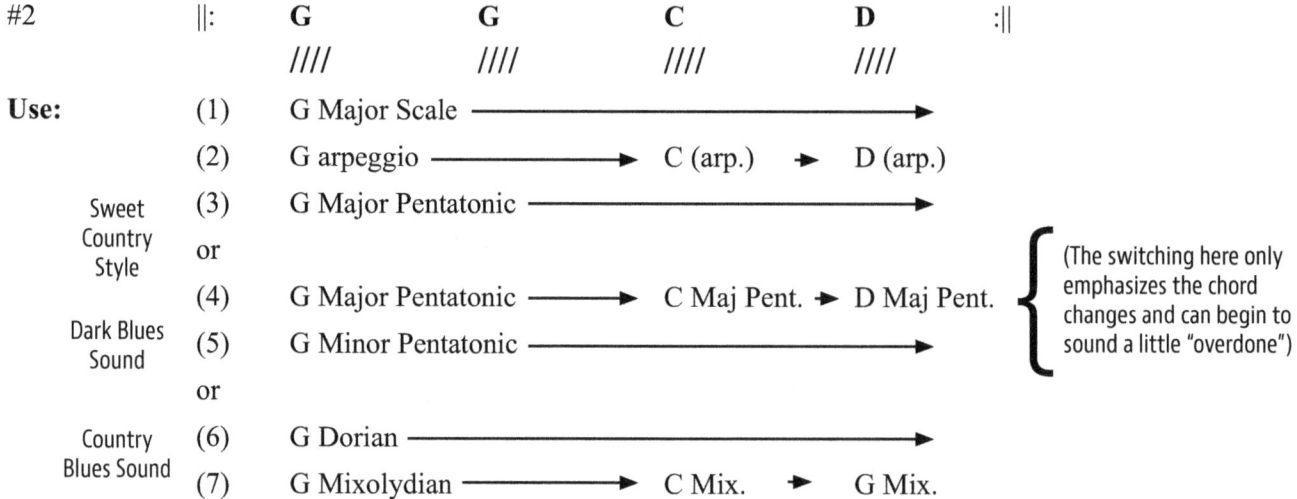

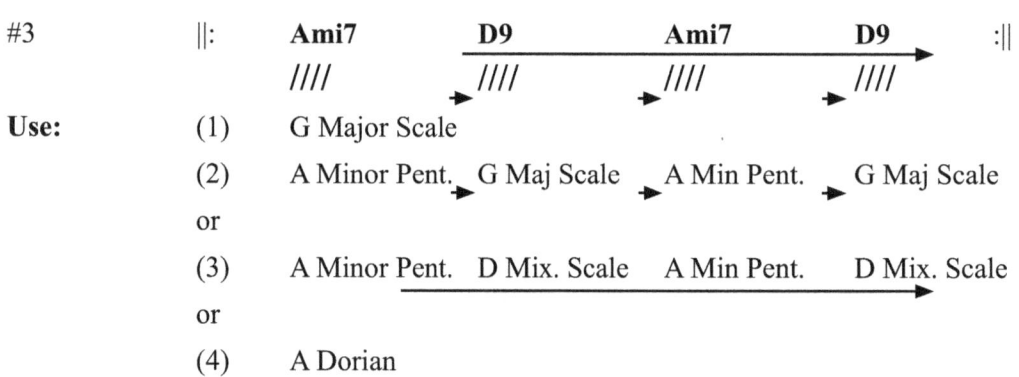

Lesson 31

Technique – Level Two

Most lessons in technique have one thing in common. In general, technique is more difficult to explain than it is to understand or play. The best way for you to understand a discussion on technique is to play it, play it, and play it! Try everything - spend time "fooling around" - what is dry and long-winded on paper can turn into a real thrill on the guitar. (That being said, I'll try not to be any longer winded than usual.)

In this lesson we are not discussing guitar playing techniques in general. We are discussing techniques used mainly in improvisation.

Part A discusses right hand techniques for "attacking" the strings, and starting and stopping sounds. Part B discusses the string bend, a function of both the left hand, and the right hand.

Part A – The Choke and the Pinch

Choke means to stop in mid-breath. Choking is a technique for single line playing. You choke a note by stopping it unexpectedly - generally right after you strike the string (when it's still vibrating loud enough to make it obvious that it has stopped). You can choke in two different ways:

1. Pick the string. Holding the pick in your right hand between your thumb and first finger, you choke the string that is sounding by resting the a) pick, b) your thumb, or c) your index finger, against the string. Try it first with the pick. Pick the string, and then bring the pick back against the string to stop it from sounding. Now repeat this over and over. Once you get some experience with this, you'll probably stop the string from ringing with the pick, thumb, and index finger, on different occasions.

2. If you're not bending a string, you can choke the note with the left hand finger that is holding down the fretted note. Simply lift your finger and the string it's pushing down, away from the fret. Do not remove your finger from the string however, or it may begin to vibrate by itself. (Not your finger - the string)

3. Pick the string, holding the pick between your thumb and fourth finger, swallow a chicken bone and laugh. If you're not choking yet, blow your nose too. (Editor: Please don't do this.)

"CHICK'N PICK'N" is a technique that starts with a choke and is then immediately followed with a normal note. Holding the pick between your thumb and first finger, grab a string between the pick and the *second* finger of your right hand. Strike the string with the pick while your second finger is still against the string (you should get a "thud"). Then strike the string with the second finger. Repeat this quickly. The sound resembles a thud followed quickly by a note. The effect is one of "stuttering." The note is played twice in a row quickly. Add different notes from the left hand, or even a string bend - that's chicken picking.

THE PINCH - If you strike the string with your pick, AND with your second finger at the same time, you are pinching the string. This is often done to get a "snap" effect and a little more volume when you want to emphasize a note.

Part B – String Bends

We've seen string bends earlier in the book when working with the major scale and arpeggios. There we introduced the basic bends as illustrated in the sketch below:

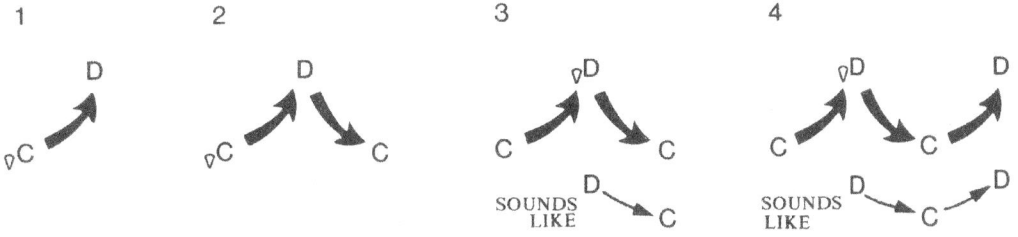

The ◊ symbol stands for the act of picking the string. The arrows signify whether you're going up or down in pitch. By "bending down" we mean slowly releasing a bent string back to its original pitch.

String Bends for the New Scales

We've seen a variety of scales and the sounds added to our basic set in the major scale. Your string bending should include all of the other notes you've added to your set of sounds. Look at the table below and using a 1e or 1a fingering shape (major or Dorian would be fine). See if you can find and bend all the notes as illustrated.

Starting Note of C Scale	C	D	Eb	E	F	Gb	G	A	Bb	B	C
1/2 Step Bends	C-Db	D-Eb 2-b3	Eb-E. b3 - 3	E -F* 3 - 4	F -Gb 4 - b5	Gb-G b5 - 5		A-Bb 6-b7			
Whole Step Bends		D-E 2.- 3	Eb -F b3 - 4	E to F#	F-G 4-5				Bb-C b7 - R		

C - Db
7b9 chord only

Eb - Gb
b3 - b5
1½Steps

*for a Csus sound only

G - Bb
5 - b7

A - C
6 - R

1½Steps

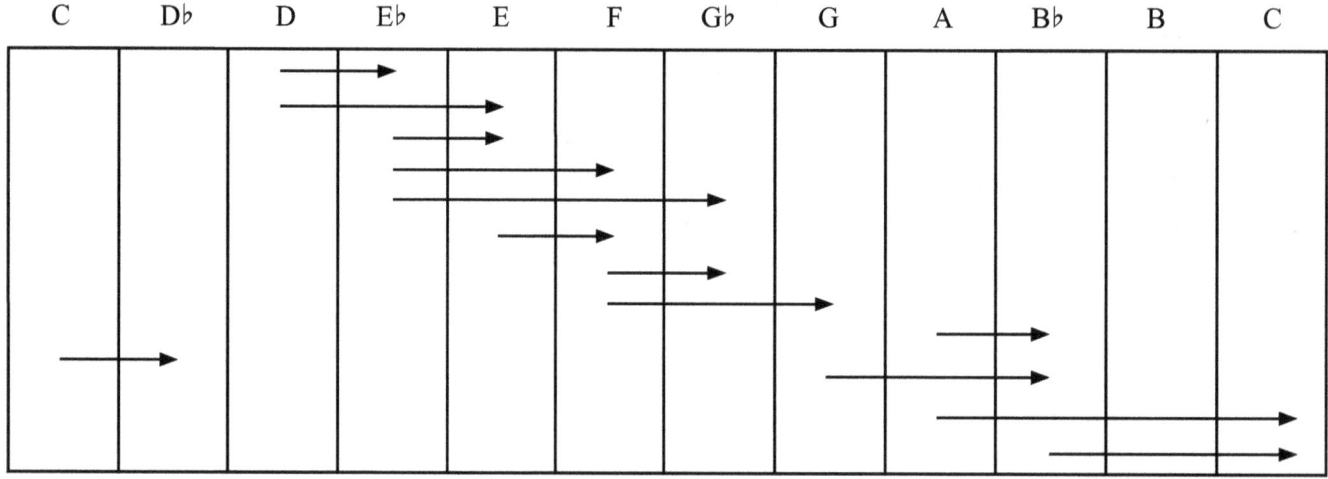

Lesson 32 - Part A

String Bends in Detail and by Position

"How do you incorporate string bends into your playing?"

The string bend is a melodic device. You use it because you are trying to communicate with it. The string bend is a tool to be put to work for you to help you express yourself. How? The area of bending strings is without limit, rule, law or restriction of application. (The only exception, which we have already mentioned, is that when you bend a string, bend it in or out of tune, but be committed. Avoid wandering, hesitant, sloppiness.) A string bend can occur at the beginning, in the middle, or at the end of "run" of notes. It can be the whole solo! Try experimenting with it in the following ways.

1. Play a major scale ascending and end it by bending the last note.
2. Begin a major scale by bending one of the high notes, and then play the scale descending.
3. Try placing a bend at the beginning or end of arpeggios in the same way as in Steps 1 and 2 above.

Where are string bends in our scale fingerings?

The string bends will be shown as they relate to scale fingerings. For this reason we will be able to show MORE THAN ONE BEND on each diagram. Below each diagram the bends will be listed by letter name, so you can be sure you're playing them all. Below is a sample, to show you this more clearly.

Remember, the fingering name tells you the position, and thus which fingers to use for bending.

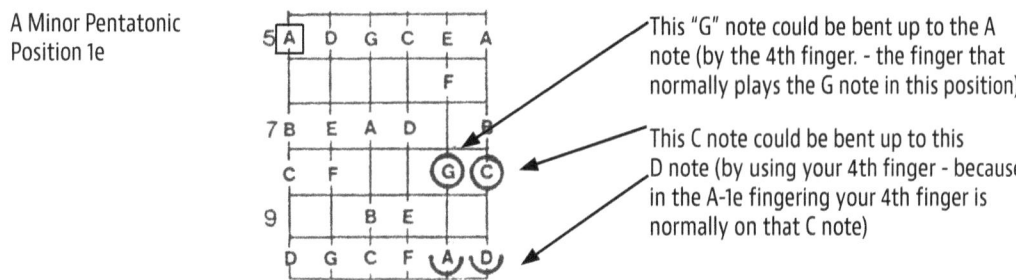

There will be several diagrams for each scale position so that there will be no confusion. Each diagram for the position will list different string bends which are possible. (We have to use several diagrams because all the bends won't fit on one!) In addition, the "Blue notes", the ♭3 and ♭7 (E♭ and B♭ in the key of C) will also be shown.

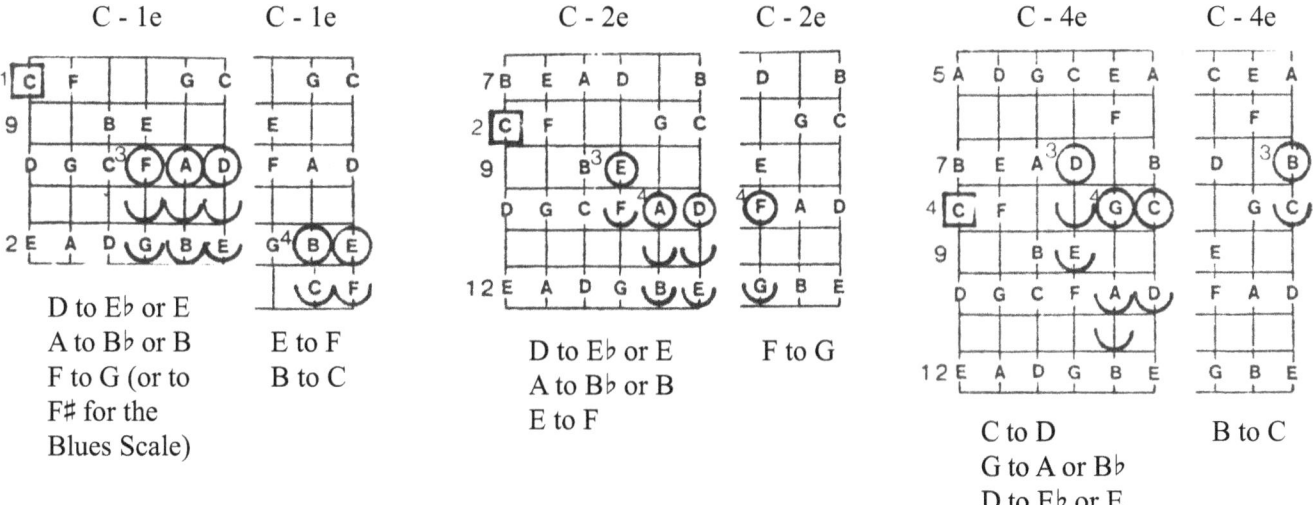

The root of the fingering position is indicated with a square on each set of diagrams.

Styles for the Studio by Leon White • 61

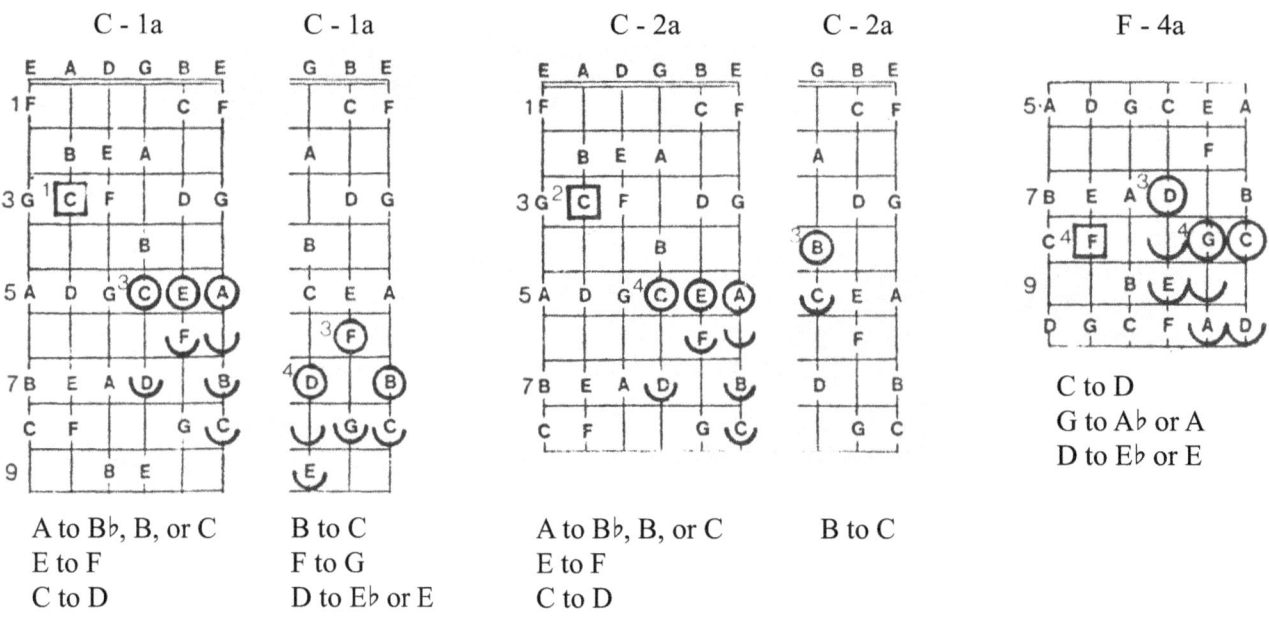

A to B♭, B, or C
E to F
C to D

B to C
F to G
D to E♭ or E

A to B♭, B, or C
E to F
C to D

B to C

C to D
G to A♭ or A
D to E♭ or E

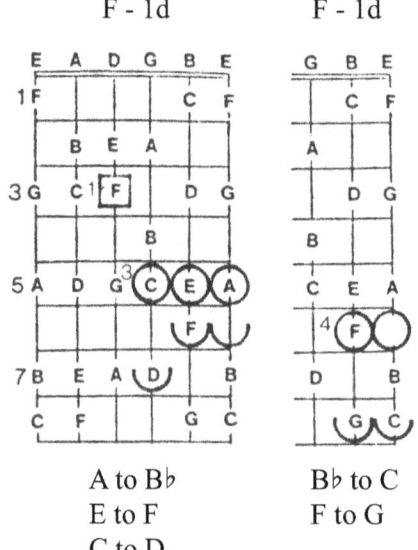

A to B♭
E to F
C to D

B♭ to C
F to G

Remember...

Practice keeping string bends **in tune**. Your best way to do this is to practice them **slowly**.

In addition, you should be trying to remember where these bends occur *in the fingerings*. Repetition will make this work out.

Where can you apply these string bends?

Most of these bends are progressional. That is, you can use them anywhere you're playing the scale. The exceptions are marked with an asterisk. These bends 1) involve a note that is pretty "far out" of the Blues Rock tonality we have become familiar with, (C, D, E♭, E, F, F♯, G, A, B♭, B, C), or 2) work especially well with only certain chords (which are noted).

To experiment with these bends, take a common progression you are familiar with and play one bend over the whole progression just to hear what it sounds like. You can use any of the sample progressions that were given with the scales so far. Repeat this for the different bends and mark the ones you like. Gradually you will develop your "ear" for string bends and this somewhat "mechanical" way of learning them will be unnecessary. However, for now it is the best way to carefully and completely investigate string bends.

Lesson 32 - Part B

String Bends and Their Relationship to Chords

We have been discussing string bends as they occur in scales, and emphasizing the relationship of the bend to notes in that scale. There is another very important consideration to be aware of — how do the notes in the bend relate to the CHORD?

This discussion is really very simple. The notes that are in the bend are either 1) contained in the chord or 2) not contained in the chord. If they are in the chord, then that's that — they harmonize exactly. If the note is NOT in the chord, then (since the note is from the scale of the chord) it is acting as a *diatonic extension* of the chord.

Watch...

C	D	E	F	G	A	B	C	D	E	F	G	A
1		3		5		7	8	9		11		13

Chords can be made by stacking every other note, from the scale. A Cma7 chord is C E G B. The remaining three notes are all diatonic extensions of the C chord. D is the 9th, F is the 11th, and A is the 13th.

We want you to analyze your string bending in terms of the STRUCTURE OF THE CHORD. For instance: given that a C7 chord is being played by the band, and you bend a C note up to a D note, what are you doing? You're bending the Root (C) to the ninth (D). It is that simple.

Doing this will help you find out which "colors" you like to use in your improvisational string bends. In addition, this kind of analysis will also help you bend from one chord into another, because it makes you think NOT in terms of scales, but in terms of chords.

Bending "Into" a Chord

Suppose you had this progression: C C F C
//// //// //// ////

Could you use your bending to emphasize the change from C to F? Yes. Bend from an E note (the third of C - C E G) to F, the root of the F chord. This is a simple example, but the principle is important. And it also shows you how important it is to know how to SPELL CHORDS. Analyze the bends illustrated below to see how they work. What do you think of the sounds?

#1	**Chords -**	C to D Major		#2	**Chords -**	C to B♭ Major
	Bends -	C to D			**Bends -**	C to D
		E to F♯				A to B♭
		G to A				E to F
#3	**Chords -**	C to G7		#4	**Chords -**	C7 to A Major
	Bends -	C to D			**Bends -**	C to C♯
		C down to B				G to A
		E to F				B down to A

Lesson 33

Harmonized Scales

This section introduces NO new melodic resources beyond the material already discussed. You have seen ALL the scales in this section already. This section shows you the following:

- How to play the "double stop" sounds (that is, technique); and
- How to organize the "double stop" sounds into your playing (how to think with harmonized scales).

As before, we'll begin our studies with the major diatonic scale. We will investigate all the "double stop" sounds with this scale before investigating the sounds in other scales.

By now you should be aware of several of the harmony and theory concepts we have mentioned, and understand the interval names "second," "third," "fourth," and so on.

In the diagram to the right there are two notes circled and connected by a straight line. These two notes should be played *together*, with one pick stroke.

As you practice Harmonized Scales, remember the following things:

1. Always use alternate picking: ↓ ↑
2. The harmonized scale fingerings are based on our original major scale fingerings.
3. In our diagrams □ indicates the Root of the scale. ○ indicates an optional note in the scale, found below the Root. Key points include the following:
4. We will show you how to experiment with string bends in harmonized scales. We'll cover bending *one of two* notes played together; and bending *both* notes played together (sometimes referred to as 'double bends.' (For a good example, you can listen to the original recording of "Midnight at the Oasis" by Maria Muldaur with a solo by guitarist Amos Garrett featuring double bends.)

How We Diagram Two Notes at Once

Since we are playing two notes at a time, we will be playing on two strings at a time. There are two ways to do this. We can play on adjacent strings, or we can play on non-adjacent strings.

Notes on Adjacent Strings

Notes on Non-Adjacent Strings

The value of these harmonized scales is that you will be able to play solos with a new, fuller sound. Instead of just one note, you will be playing two notes at a time. In addition, playing these harmonized lines is the first step in being able to "comp" behind singers or other soloists.

To the right is the special diagram which we will use to simplify our work. These diagrams break up the six strings on the guitar into pairs of two adjacent strings. There is also a version showing three adjacent strings.

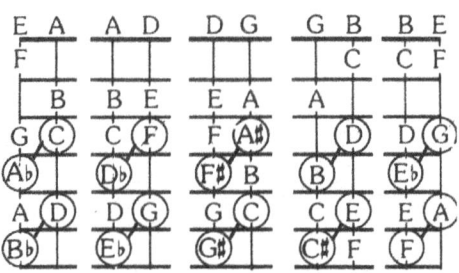

Styles for the Studio by Leon White • 64

Technique

There are several different techniques used in playing these two-note sounds. Both your left hand and your right hand will be doing new things, so we have put some exercises in the beginning of this part to help you eliminate some of your initial awkwardness. These introductory exercises will focus on the two main problems:

1. Picking two adjacent strings with one stroke of your right hand (up or down), and
2. Fretting two adjacent strings with any one of your four left hand fingers

You must be able to do both of these things rapidly and with ease if you are to become good at playing "double stops." The following exercises will help you develop your dexterity, so that the fingerings for the harmonized scales will be easier to play.

> *Of all the material I've taught and written, these exercises are perhaps the most powerful and effective technique tools I've ever shared. They help your playing way beyond their use for double string dexterity.*
>
> *I learned them from guitarist Mike Warren and I still play them as warm ups. They help calibrate your feel to the instrument (especially useful if you switch instruments often); and they help with two-hand coordination. They also work the right hand in control and tone. These are gold. ~LW*

Exercise 1: Play the notes in pairs. Play the G-C♯ pair and then the A-D♯ pair. Repeat this on the other sets of strings as shown. You can also reverse this exercise by playing the A-D♯ pair FIRST (and playing the G-C♯ pair second).

Exercises 2, 3, 4, 5, 6, and 7: Play each of these exercises as you did Exercise 1. Do not skip these!! They are super chop builders. (As opposed to "supper-chops" I guess.)

Fingering: For all of these exercises, your first finger plays the notes on the third fret; your second finger plays notes on the fourth; your third plays notes on the fifth, and your fourth finger plays notes on the sixth fret. (As shown in Ex. 2.)

I also play these examples as single line warm-ups. It amounts to alternate picking on alternate strings all the way across the fingerboard.

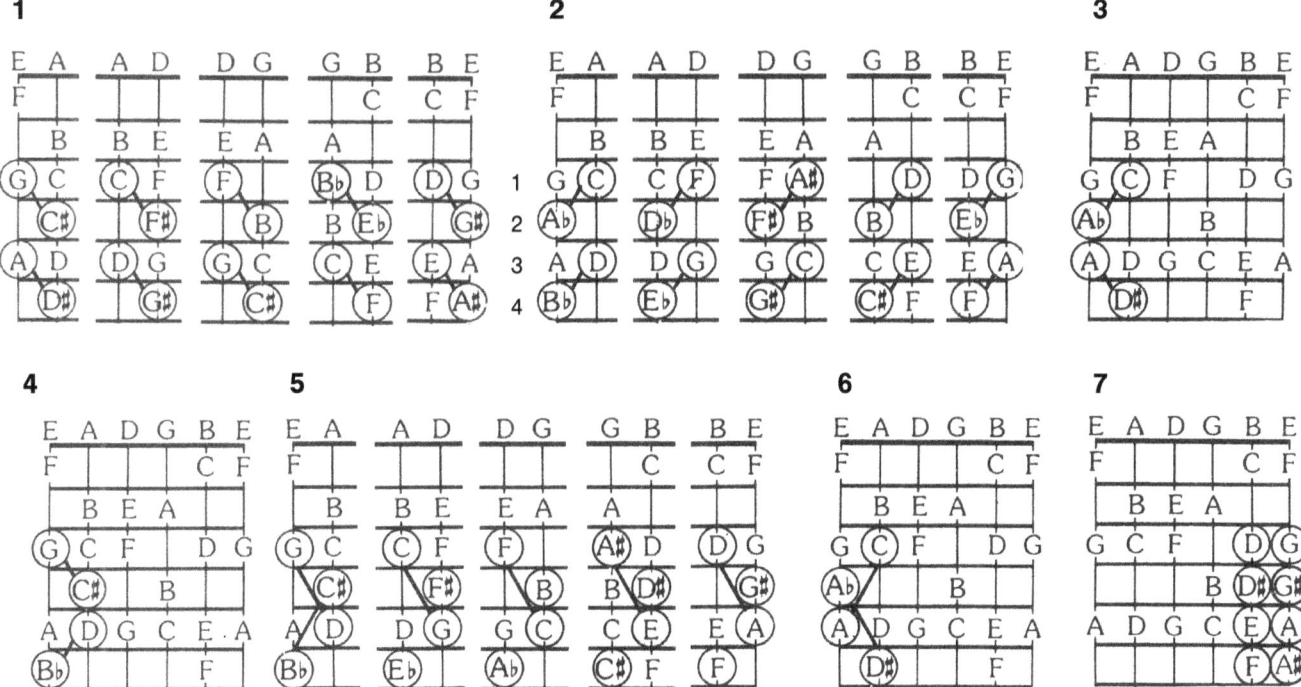

Styles for the Studio by Leon White

Lesson 34

The Major Scale in Thirds

Our first effort will be to harmonize the major scale in thirds. After the thirds, we will study the scale in 4ths and 6ths. The fingerings all follow the original fingerings we used for the major scale. Please take your time in memorizing these fingerings; you will only be able to "rip through" them when you *really* know them. (Remember, in a few pages we're going to start bending strings with these . . .) This section is a lot of fun; Good luck!

NOTE: Try leaving out parts of these fingerings - you can find some interesting sounds - for instance: in the following examples we have shown the complete fingering on the left, and the shortened version on the right. Also please note that not *all* of the original fingerings can be played in thirds - there are only five, in fact.

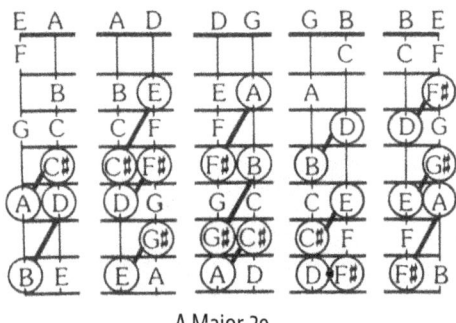
A Major 2e

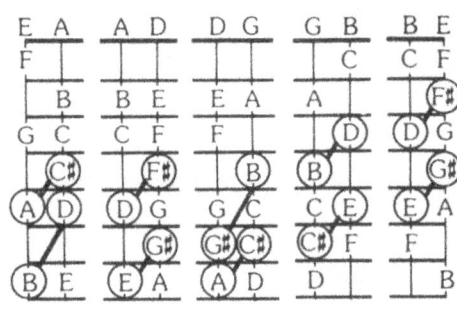
A Major 2e Shortened

All fingerings given here are optional - if you prefer others, write them in

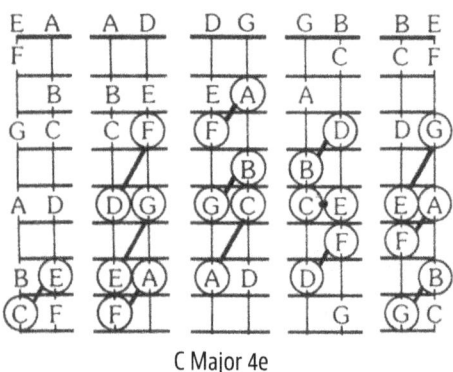
C Major 4e

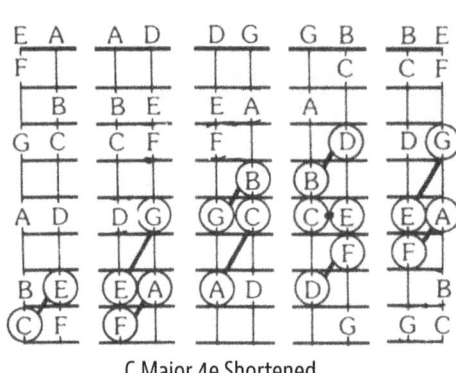
C Major 4e Shortened

F Major 2a

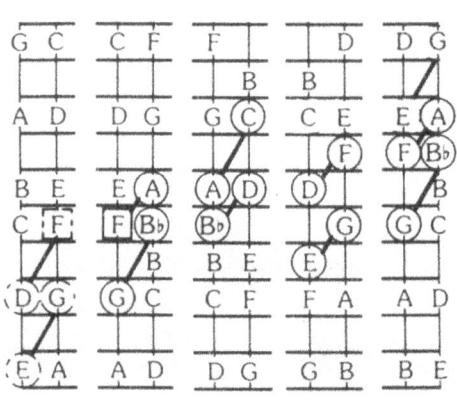
F Major 2a Shortened

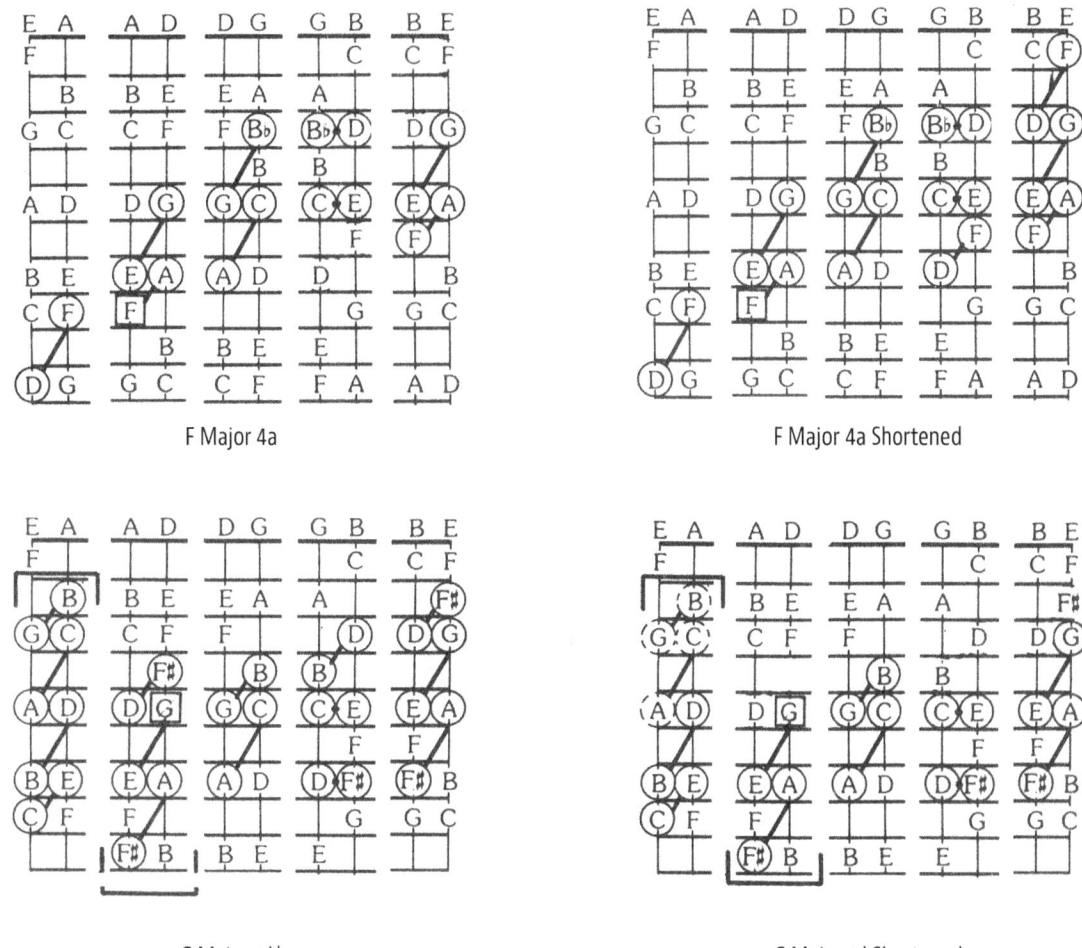

F Major 4a

F Major 4a Shortened

G Major 1d*

G Major 1d Shortened

* Please note that you can start down on the low G note, and play up that low pair of strings, if you want to hear the scale from its root. (We've indicated this on the diagram in a bracket: [ ])

Special Fingering Considerations

Most people find sliding between note pairs easier to play, *at first*. However there is a serious drawback - sliding sounds like sliding. The notes tend to be slurred together. There is nothing wrong with this sound itself, but if you only know this one technique, then you cannot develop the notes as separate independent sounds. A second drawback is speed. With some practice you should be able to play the notes as fingered in the shortened versions faster. (You will also have the advantage of being able to hammer them on.)

Another consideration to be noted is that sliding takes you out of position, making it a little more difficult to play without looking at your guitar.

In addition to the points mentioned above, certain sequences of notes will 'feel' good played in one fingering descending, and in another ascending. This will also occur as you begin improvising with harmonized scales- bending strings, hammering on notes, leaving pairs of notes out, and so on.

This discussion is to call your attention to the fingering. Try our fingering first, and if it feels peculiar, or you prefer to slide all the time then write in your own fingerings. In any event, *stop and think* about the fingerings as you begin to study and use the harmonized scales.

How Can You Use Harmonized Major Scales?

You can play a harmonized major scale anywhere you can play a regular major scale. Try the following progressions with a C harmonized scale.

Be sure you are always using alternate picking here! To help you practice this picking, try the harmonized scales by starting out on an "up" stroke instead of a "down" stroke, and play alternating strokes from there.

#1 Dmi7 G7 Dmi7 G7 Dmi7 G7 Cma7 Cma7
  //// //// //// //// //// //// //// ////

#2 Emi7 Ami7 Dmi7 G7 Cma7 Cma7
  //// //// //// //// //// ////

#3 Bmi7♭5 Ami7 Dmi7 Cma7
  //// //// //// ////

#4 Fma7 Fma7 Emi7 Ami7 Dmi7 G7 Fma7 B7 Cma7
  //// //// //// //// //// //// //// //// ////

(That B7 should have sounded hideous - I was just checking to see if you're asleep here or not – Virginia's father snored on.)

#5 Cma7 Dmi7 Emi7 Dmi7
  //// //// //// ////

#6 Go back to any of the progressions used earlier in the book, and try the harmonized scales there.

If you're still having trouble getting these scales to sound "clean" — practice the technique exercises more slowly, and be patient. The sound will get cleaner as you play them more.

Lesson 35 - Part A

The Major Scale in Fourths and Sixths

This lesson will explore the sounds and fingerings used when harmonizing the major scale in fourths and sixths. The harmonized fourths are a common sound for "pop ballad" fills and in a number of Motown arrangements. The sixths are familiar to you from country-rock and traditional country music.

Your right hand technique for the 'fourths' can be the alternate flat picking we have been using because the notes are on adjacent strings.

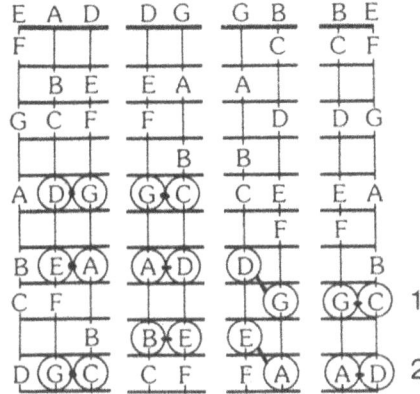
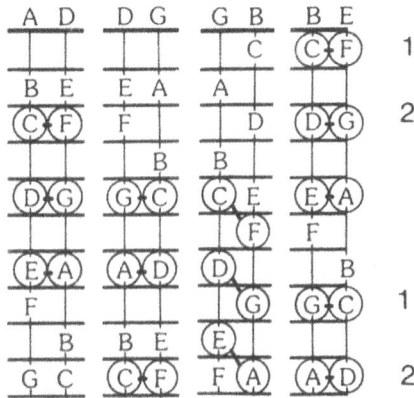

Play these 'fourths' over C major type chords. Start with the pairs on the treble strings.

Always use alternate picking with pairs of notes like #1. Fret both notes with one finger (group #1 with your first finger, group #2 with your third).

To get the sound try the following hints:

1. Slide up and back between close pairs of notes. For instance - slide #1 up to #2 and back again with any of the pairs numbered #1 and #2 in the above diagrams.

2. Alternate pairs of notes - play the pairs in this order: 1st pair, 2nd pair, 1st pair.

3. Play "down" through the groups of fourths as shown in the diagrams below

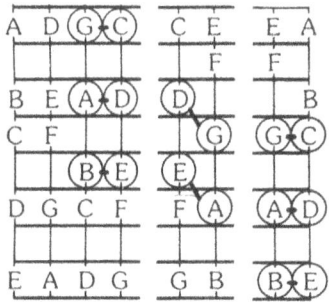
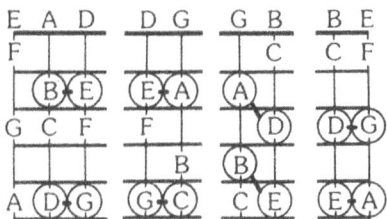

Styles for the Studio by Leon White

Lesson 35 - Part B

Playing the Major Scale in Sixths

C	D	E	F	G	A	B	C
1	2	3	4	5	6		
	1	2	3	4	5	6	

C to A is a sixth
D to B is a sixth

The interval of a sixth is a very consonant interval, and is used frequently in country and country-rock styles of music. You'll also hear guitarists like Steve Cropper use them to create memorable introductions and fills on many recordings. Because sixths are seen most often on NON ADJACENT STRINGS, there are several new ways to play them.

1. You can play these two notes simultaneously. To do this, strike the lower pitched note with your flat pick, in the normal fashion (with a down stroke). At the same time pluck the other note with the second finger of your right hand (this plucking motion should be towards the ceiling).

2. You can play the notes one *after* the other, and you can do this starting with either note. Use the same motions to strike the strings as described in step one above. However, instead of making both motions at the same time, play them one AFTER the other. Remember, you can pluck the high string first, and then pick the lower note, or you can pick the low note first, and then pluck the higher one.

3. There is also another technique for playing the notes one after the other. Because we are not playing the notes together, we can strike BOTH notes with the pick. Picking here is optional. To get started we suggest down on the lower note first, and up on the higher note afterwards.

How the Diagrams Work

To illustrate sixths we are going to be using the TRIGRAM(©*1976 Leon R. White*). Each group of strings is called a STRINGSET. We will show sixths in scale fingerings and out of scale fingerings, using all of the string sets, with the fingerings indicated on each diagram. (See below)

How to practice sixths:

1. EXPERIMENT WITH THEM - try to find sounds you recognize from records and recordings.

2. Practice playing the sixths in the scale fingerings shown, against chord progressions. We will show you some progressions that you may use.

Styles for the Studio by Leon White • 70

Shown below is one set of four Trigrams. Each string set shows a different major scale in sixths. To play, start on any string set, and staying on that set alone, play up the neck (in the direction of the arrow). Do you see that there is a certain pattern in the fingering? Play #4 from the first fret, and from the eighth (at the C note).

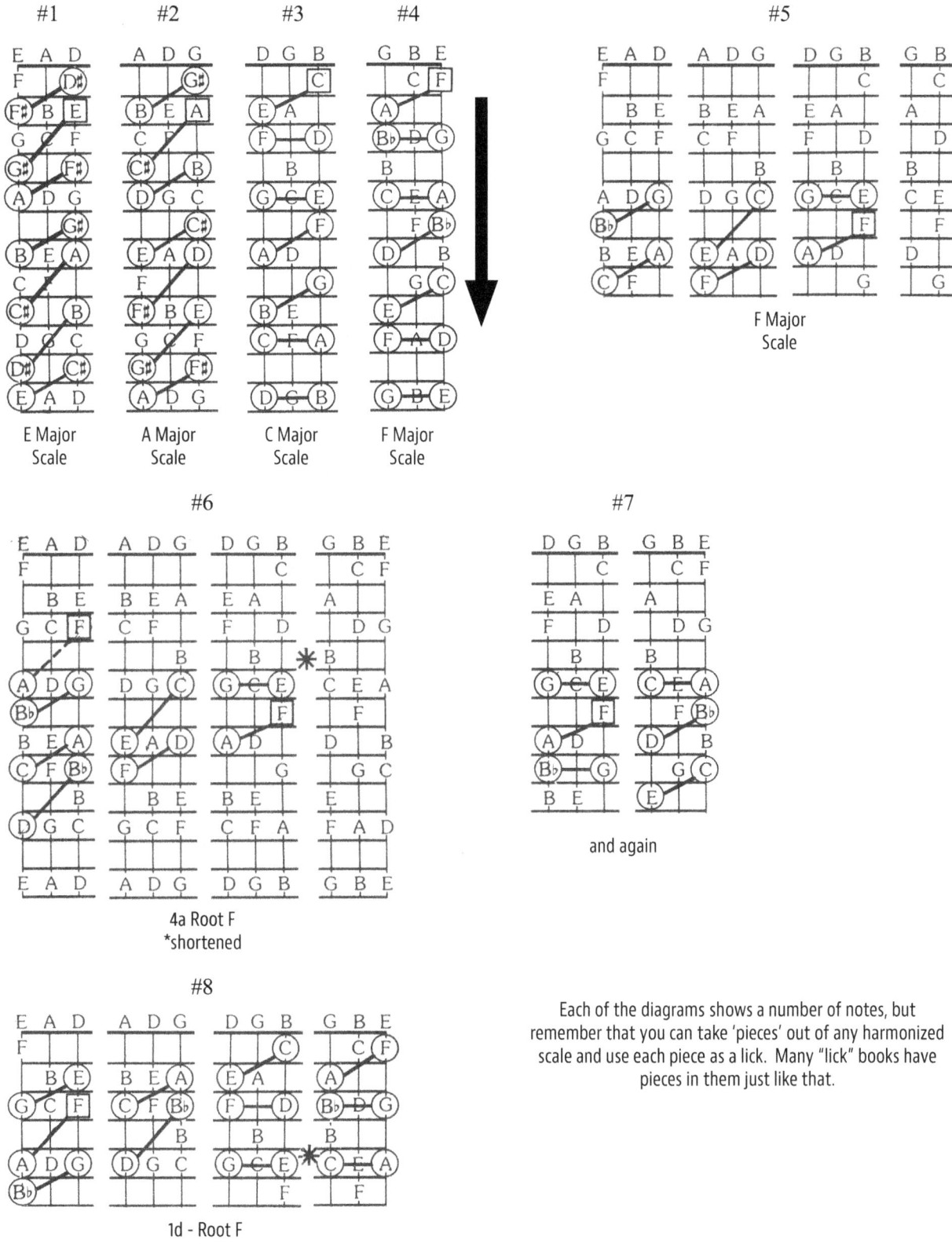

Each of the diagrams shows a number of notes, but remember that you can take 'pieces' out of any harmonized scale and use each piece as a lick. Many "lick" books have pieces in them just like that.

Examples 5, 6 and 7 all show one fingering, played in different parts or shortened.

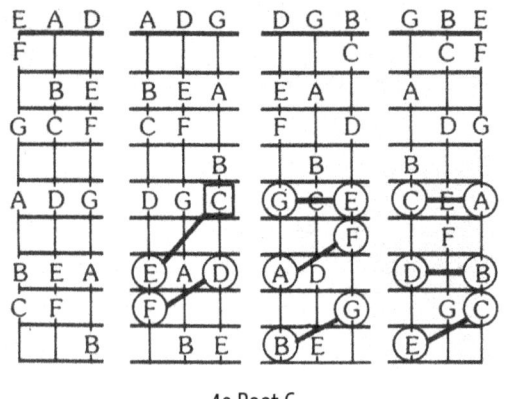
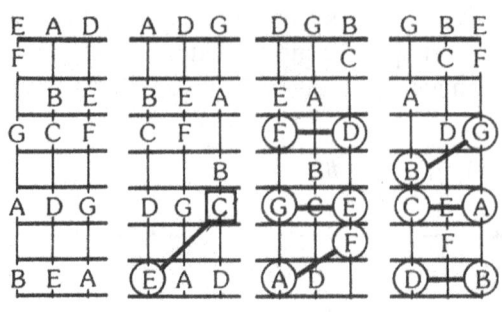

4e Root C 3e Root C

We are calling your attention to the two fingerings above to show you how you should be thinking and questioning as you learn fingerings. These sixths can appear to wander all over the fingerboard, so it's important for you to be able to visualize them and hear them. This is especially true when moving them to new keys (like B♭ Major for example). How will you finger these? Find the fingering that can be clean, clear, fast, and may have some hammer-ons.

Using "SIXTHS" of a Scale with Different Chords

Let's take the chords in a progression example:

#1 C   C   G7   C   These chords are in the key of C Major.
   //// //// //// ////

You would choose to use a C Major scale for your sixths. For the chords, try beginning with a pair of notes which had a chord tone as the highest note in that pair. (See example 2 for the C chord and example 3 for the G7 chord.)

You can move up or down in the scale from these points, in any sequence or combination. The important thing is to emphasize the chord change, by playing a note from the chord as part of the "sixth" pair. Let your ear guide you.

As an option you could move to the G major scale for sixths over the G7, but beware - the F♯ note may clash.

#2 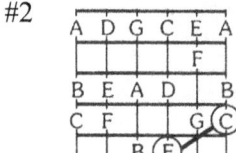   #3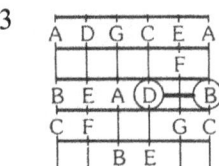

#4 C   C   B♭   B♭
   //// //// //// ////

The easiest way to think in this situation, is to imagine each chord is a I chord in its own key. If you did this, you would then play sixths from the C scale for the C chord, and sixths from the B♭ scale for the B♭ chord.

#5 Am   Am   D9   D9   (Both of these chords belong to the key of G Major
   //// //// //// ////   - D9 is a diatonic extension of D7)

Because both of these chords are in the same key, you could play sixths from the scale of that key; here it is G.

Remember: If the chords are all in the same key, use sixths from that key. Try to find sixths that include or emphasize chord tones from the different chords.

If the chords are in different keys, you can use sixths from the scale of each key, as in the example above. Once again try to emphasize chord tones - this will help you to hear the harmonization more easily, as well as helping to define the progression of chords for the listener.

Lesson 36

Harmonizing Scales Other Than the Diatonic Major Scale

This lesson is going to show you all the fingerings used to harmonize the Dorian and Mixolydian scales (in the same fashion as they were shown for the Diatonic Major). However, because the process is identical to that which you have already seen, we will omit the explanation.

The Dorian Scale in Thirds

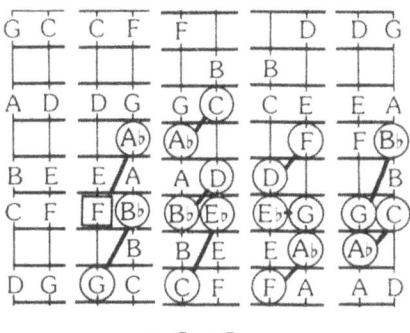

3a Root F

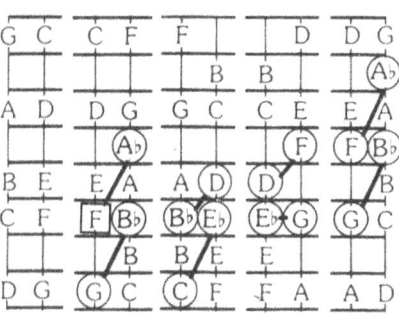

3a Root F shortened

From now on we will omit fingerings for most examples. Only at points of possible confusion will they be included. You should be experimenting, investigating and making up your own mind.

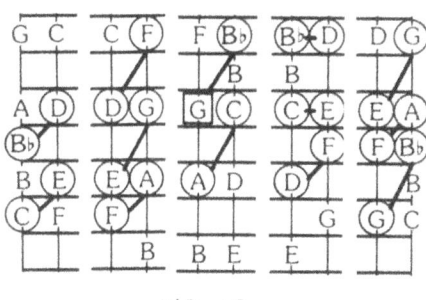

1d Root G

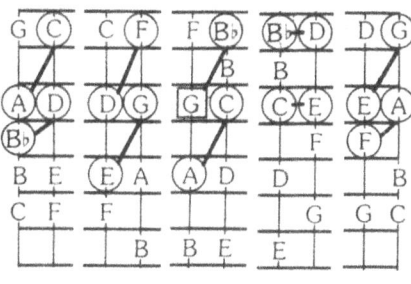

1d Root G shortened

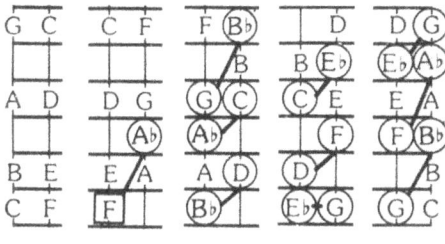

4a Root F

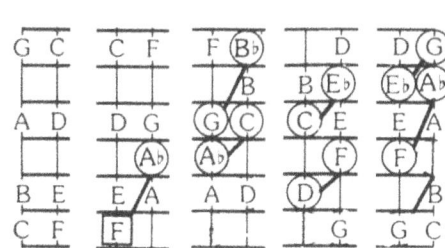

4a Root F shortened

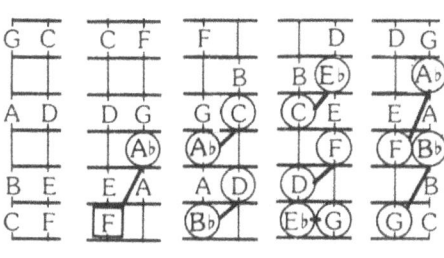

4a Root F shortened

Remember to reverse your alternate picking - start with an up stroke instead of a down. Also - on occasion you may find a fingering you prefer to what we have shown - write it in.

Lesson 37

Dorian Scale in Thirds

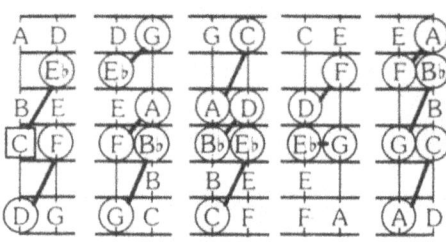

3e - Root C

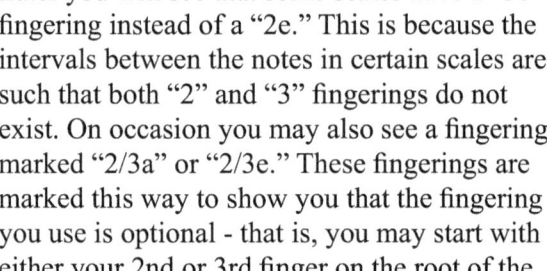

3e - Root C Shortened

Special Note

Later you will see that some scales have a "3e" fingering instead of a "2e." This is because the intervals between the notes in certain scales are such that both "2" and "3" fingerings do not exist. On occasion you may also see a fingering marked "2/3a" or "2/3e." These fingerings are marked this way to show you that the fingering you use is optional - that is, you may start with either your 2nd or 3rd finger on the root of the scale.

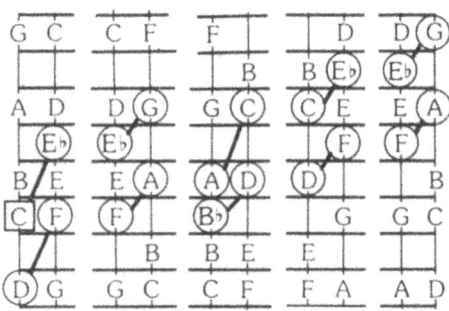

3e – Root C shortened

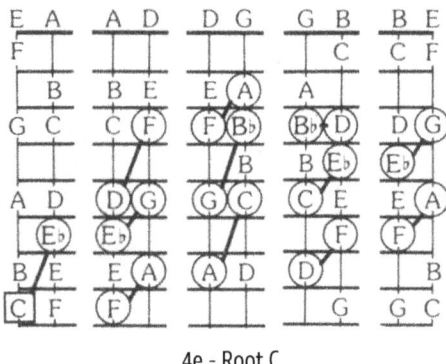

4e - Root C

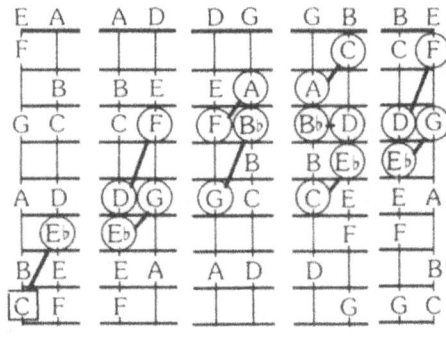

4e - Root C Shortened

Dorian Scale in Sixths

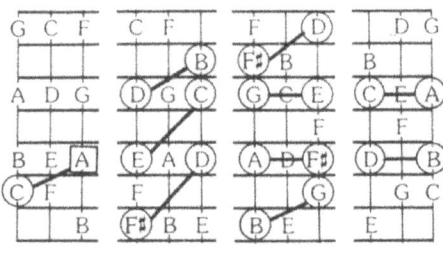

1e – Root A

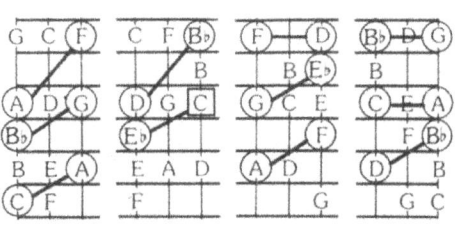

1a – Root C

Styles for the Studio by Leon White • 74

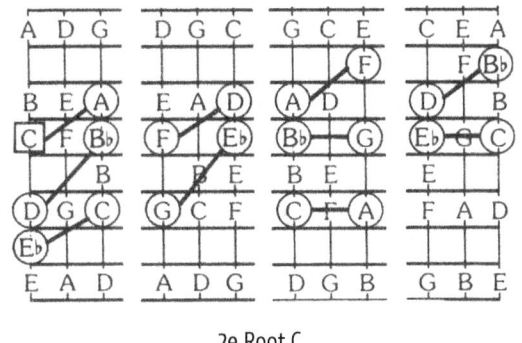

2e Root C

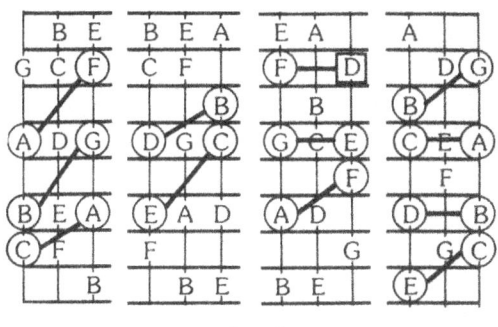

2a Root D

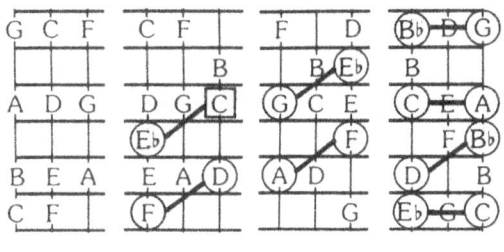

4e Root C

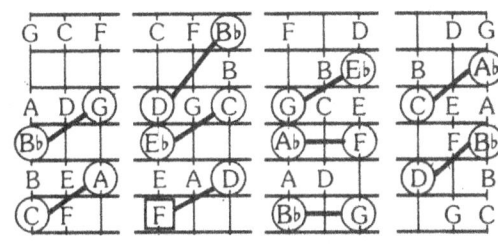

4a Root F

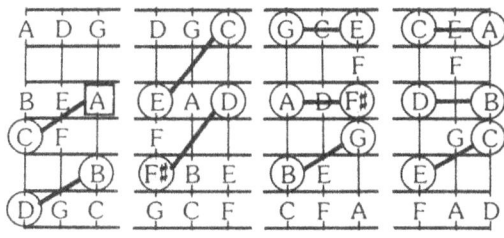

1d Root A

As before, watch your fingering!

Remember: Sixths are pairs of notes. They can be played simultaneously, or the notes in each pair can be played one after the other, (low then high or high then low).

The Mixolydian Scale in Thirds

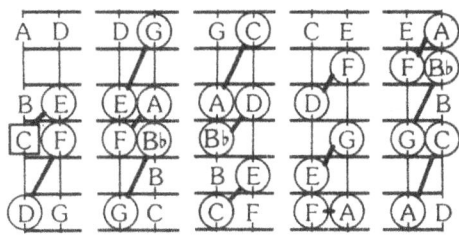

2e Root C

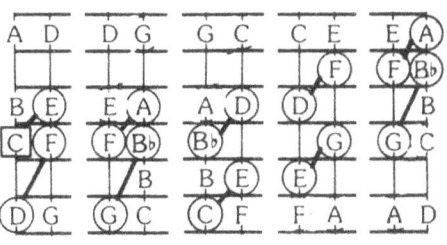

2e Root C Shortened

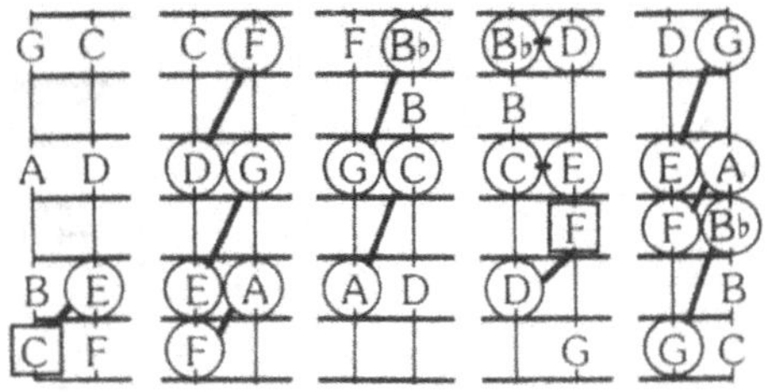

4e Root C

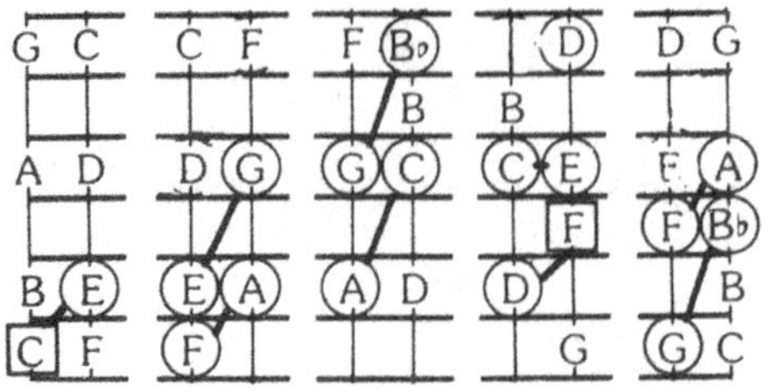

4e Root C Shortened

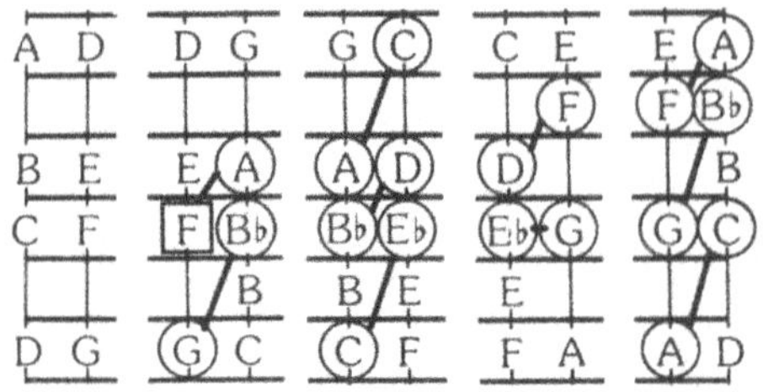

2a Root F

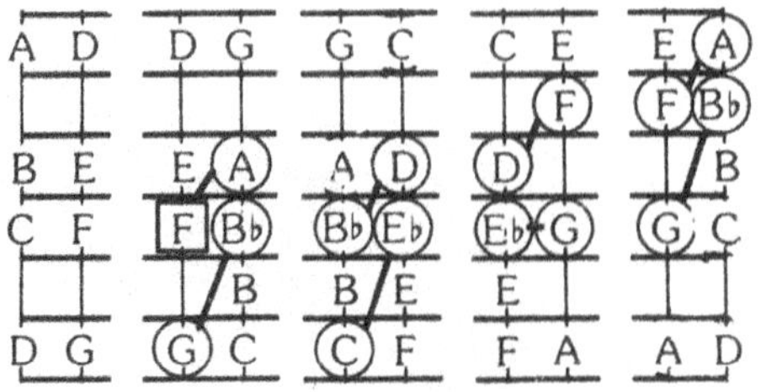

2a Root F Shortened

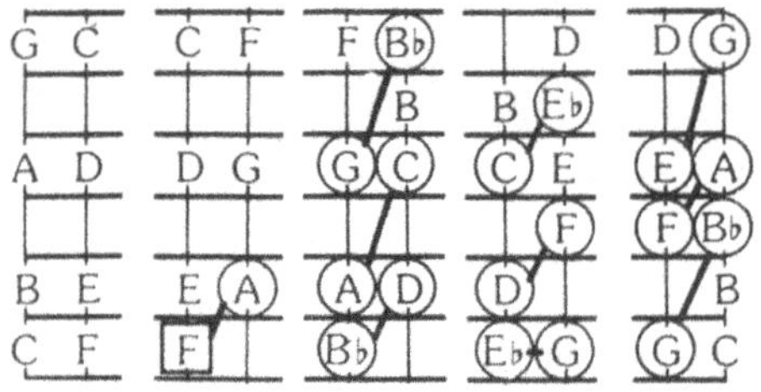

4a Root F

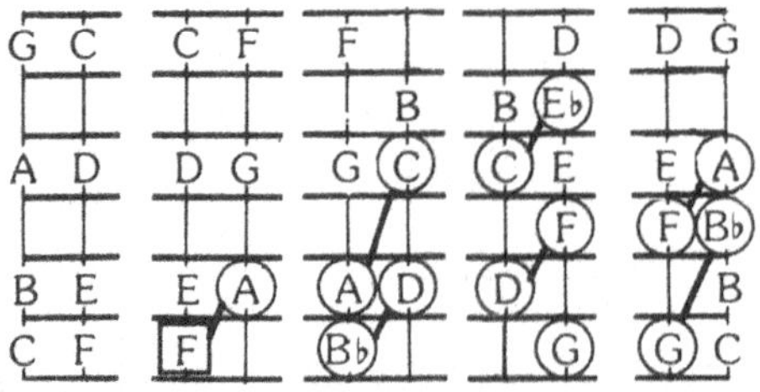

4a Shortened

The shortened versions are included to show you how the scale may be turned into potential riff material by simply leaving something out. Also, two sets of notes per string set allows you to pick quickly, and play right across the strings.

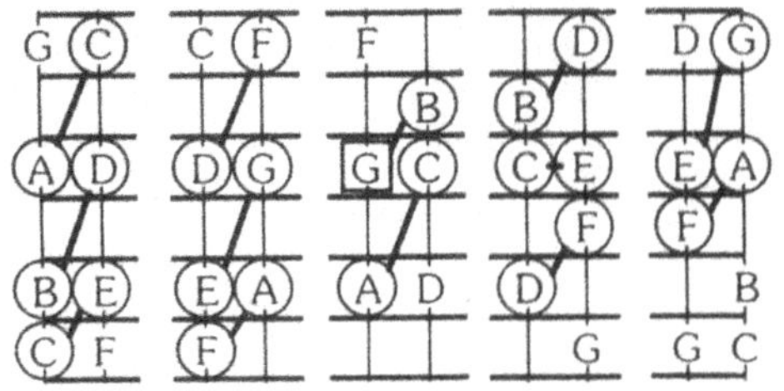

2d Root G

The Mixolydian Scale in Sixths

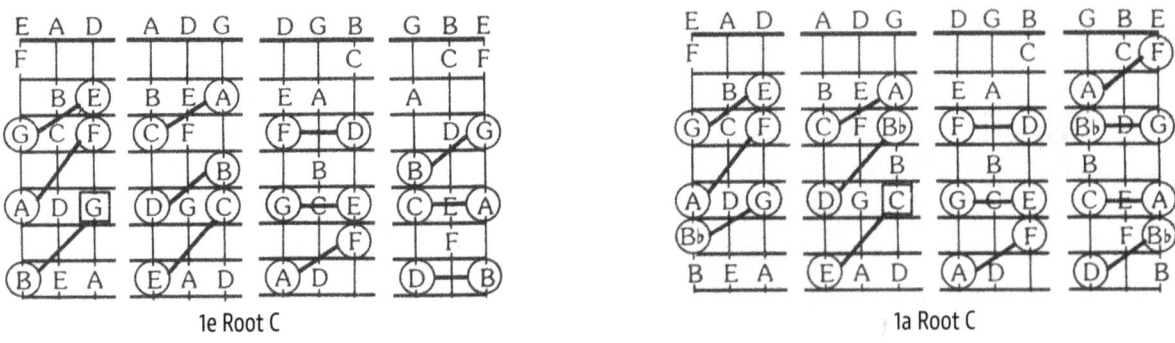

1e Root C

1a Root C

Styles for the Studio by Leon White • 76

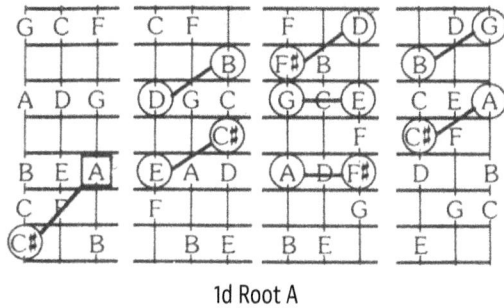

1d Root A

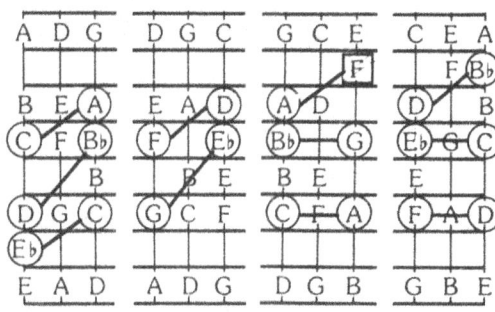

1a Root F

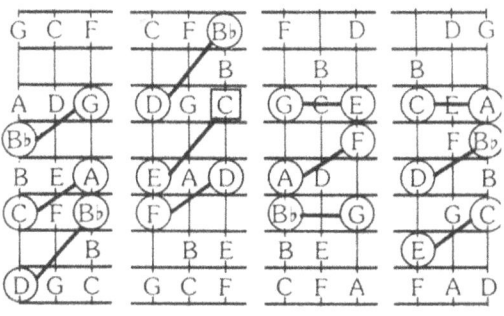

2e Root C

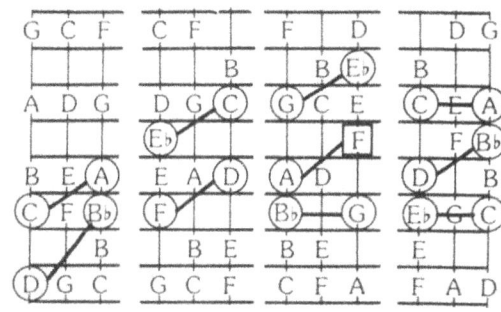

2e Root C Shortened

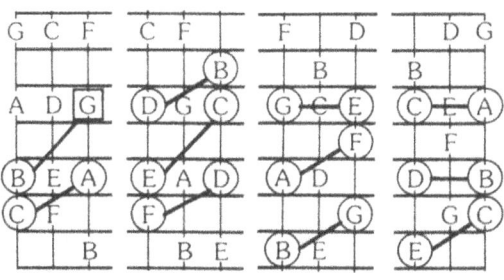

1d Root G

Because the pentatonics have only five notes, they do not lend themselves to this kind of harmonization. The blues scale is also difficult to harmonize because of its odd interval construction. We did discuss them in bending discussions however.

Lesson 38

Bending Strings in the Harmonized Scale Patterns

String bends will occur in two different ways:
- The strings you're working with will be adjacent to each other. Or ...
- The strings will be NON adjacent.

Because this lesson is organized by fingerings, you will see both kinds of bends (adjacent and NON adjacent together). It is also important to note that because of the nature of the guitar and your hand, you will be bending the lower of the two notes.

Bending follows our general rules.

1. Bend from one note in the scale to another note, *in that scale* (Generally a half-step, whole step, or step and one half).
2. Bend in *tune*.
3. Remember, you can bend up or "down."

Below is the diagram we will use to show string bends. The circled notes are a pair of notes from the harmonized scale. The note with the "cup" on it is the note being bent up to.

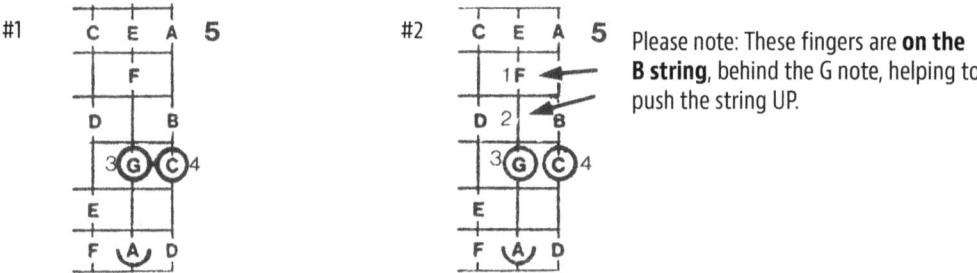

Because bending strings requires some strength, it may take a little while for you to get used to it. Because of the strength needed, the pair of notes involved in a bend may occasionally be fingered differently than they appear in the harmonized scale.

Fingerings will be indicated. If you have trouble pushing up the string with one finger, try adding another finger or two behind it. (See Diag. 2.) This technique will be used extensively - so start practicing it now. The additional fingers allow you much more control, as well as making it easier. We will also use this technique in most of the double bend situations coming up soon. .

We have organized string bends by scale interval so that we may be sure that, as we investigate all these new sounds, we don't accidentally omit something of value. We want to be absolutely sure that we try all of the possible sounds.

In these diagrams the note NOT being Bent will be in a square (□). The note being bent will be circled, (○) with the pitch you're bending up to, cupped (∪). The note held will be from the chord, while the note being bent will be from the scale. (Please note - in the key of C it is a C chord we're holding. In the key of F it is an F chord.)

The string bends will be shown as they relate to scale fingerings. For this reason we will be able to show MORE THAN ONE BEND on each diagram. Below each diagram the bends will be listed by letter name, so you can be sure you're playing them all. Look at the sample to see how this will be shown.

The bends will be shown only on the strings they occupy. Look at the complete scale fingering shown to the left, to locate the bend.

The example:

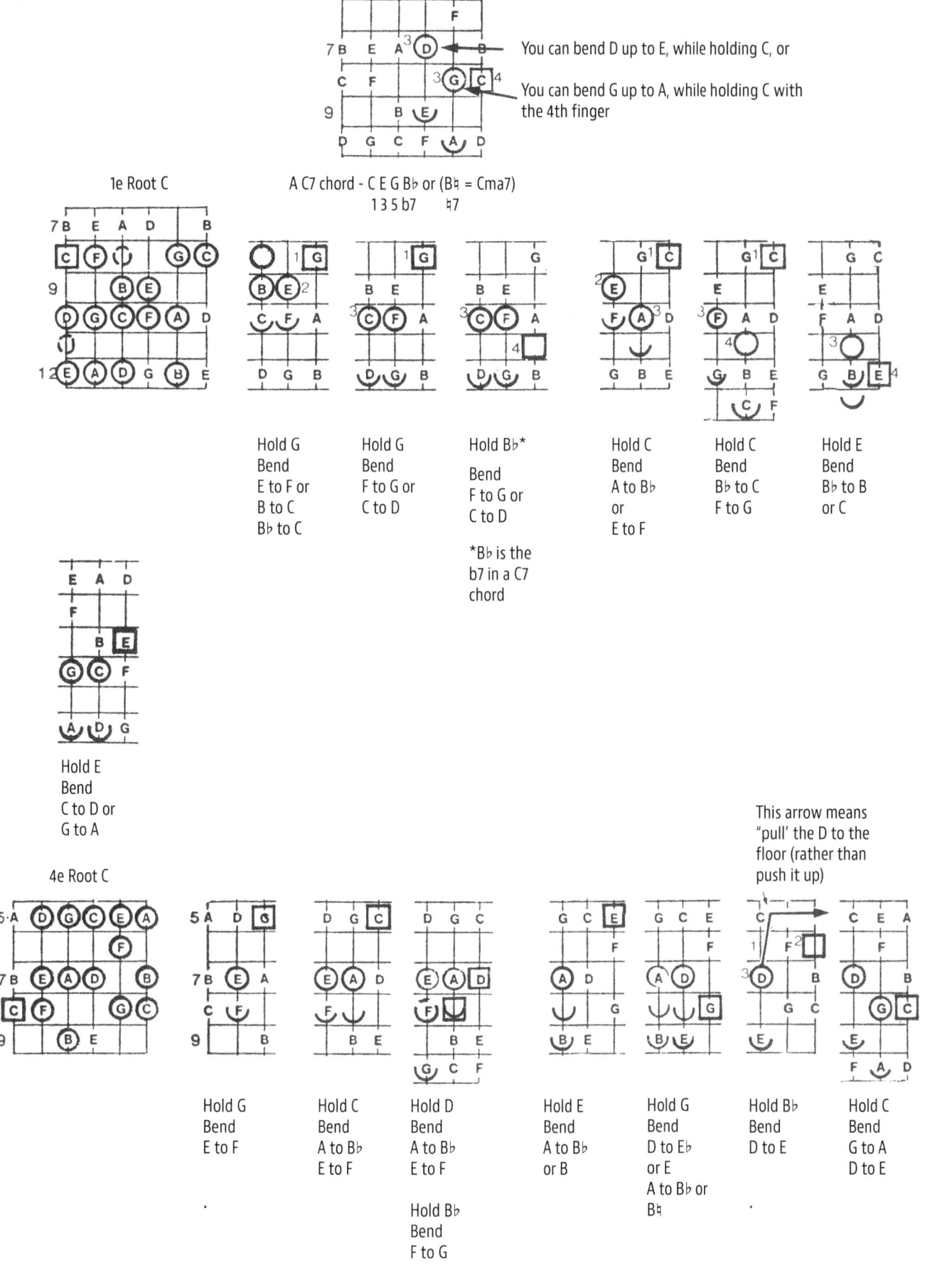

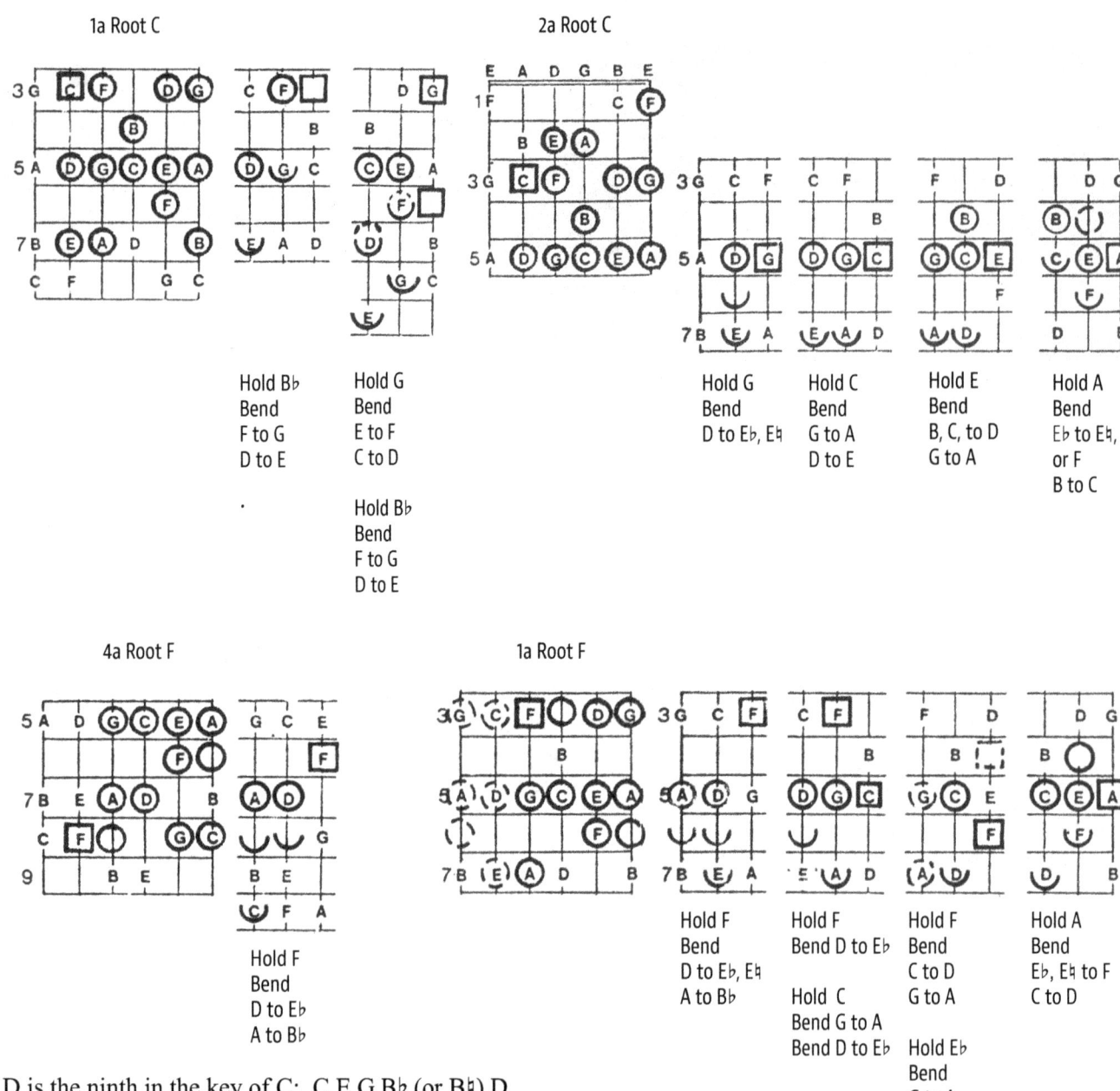

D is the ninth in the key of C: C E G B♭ (or B♮) D
1 3 5 ♭7 (or ♮7) 9

Please note that many bends work in more than one key (and scale). Compare 4a-F, with 4e-C.

Bending into Another Chord

While we have been dealing with notes all in the same scale, and which can therefore "work" with most (if not all) of the chords of that scale, there is another "effect" that is worth noting. You can bend from one chord into a *new chord*.

The notes that you start with should harmonize with your starting chord; the notes you end with after the bend should harmonize with the new chord. For instance: The bend in Diagram #1 would work with the following chord changes (among others).

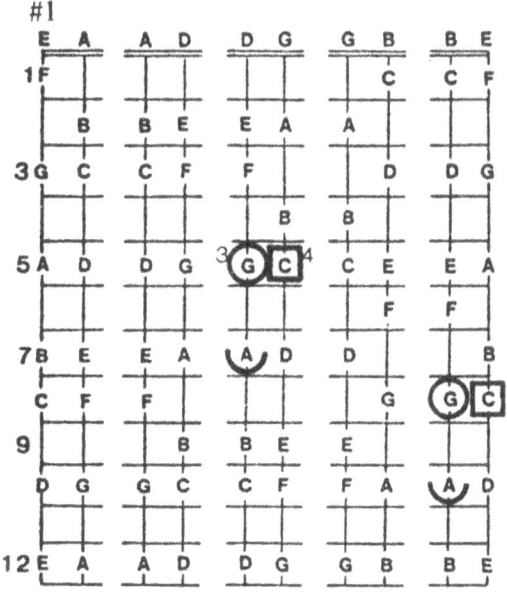

C7	to	D7
CEGB♭	to	DF♯AC
C7	to	Fma7 (or F7)
		FACE, FACE♭
C7	to	Ami7
		ACEG
C7	to	C6
		CEGA

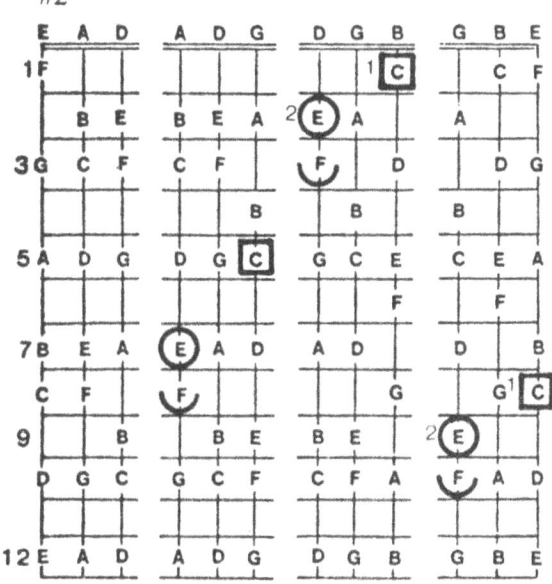

Diagram #2 would work with this change:

Cma7	or	C7	to	Fma7
CEGB		CEGB♭		FACE

```
C       F
 ↗
E       A
 ↘ ↘
G       C
```

The C note is held and the E note is bent up to the F note.

How about Ami7 to D9? You could hold a high A note and bend the E note below it to F♯. Review the harmonized scales and start experimenting!

Lesson 39

Bending Two Strings at Once

Bending two strings at once (double stop bending) may be completely new to you. Don't panic! It is not as hard as it seems, and is the source of many exciting sounds. How do you learn "double bends?"

1. Play the two notes you are beginning the bend from.
2. Now FRET the two notes you are trying to bend up to. Do not bend anything here — just listen to the sound of the notes fretted, that is, as they SHOULD SOUND when you have completed the bend correctly.
3. Now go back to the original notes — finger them as shown on the diagram. Pick the two strings at the same time, and bend them (push them up towards the ceiling).

Try to make the notes that are sounding now, sound like the two notes you fretted in step #2. The first time you try this, it will sound strange, and probably not in tune. Just keep trying. And check yourself by repeating steps 1 and 2 as you practice. Double bending is a unique and exciting sound, which CAN be done if you just work at it. There are many professional players who use double bends all the time - You can too! Double bends only sound 'right' when both string bends are really in tune. If you can play the example, read on.

4. After you have tried steps 1, 2, and 3, try this: instead of picking the notes and THEN bending them, bend them first, and then pick them as you UNBEND them. When done correctly, this should sound like two notes miraculously sliding down to two other notes. It is a good "pedal steel" effect!
5. To get even more exotic, try Step 4 and pick the strings one at a time. With both strings bent, pick one string and then release it. Then pick and release the second string in the same way (use the example for this).

Remember, notes and PAIRS OF NOTES can be in different scales, and work with more than one chord.

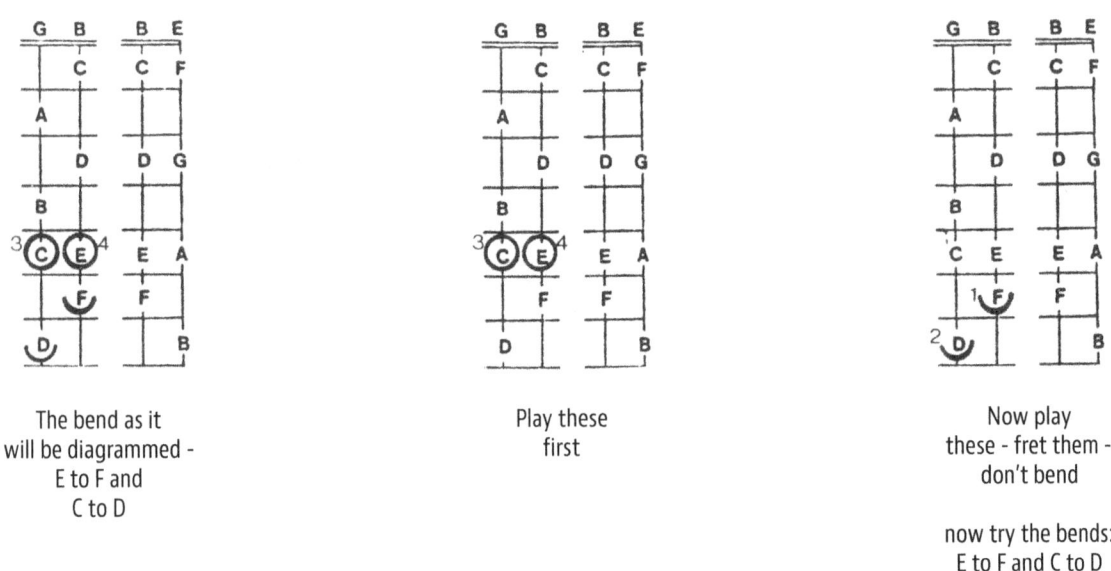

The bend as it will be diagrammed -
E to F and
C to D

Play these
first

Now play
these - fret them -
don't bend

now try the bends:
E to F and C to D

Special Technique Note: Double string bends require that you take special care in your left hand fingerings, and MOTIONS. It is absolutely essential that you keep your fingers well arched, and play and bend with the tips (and NOT the sides). In addition, certain bends on the lower strings will require you to PULL the strings (to the floor) rather than push (to the ceiling). These bends will be diagrammed with a large arrow to remind you of this. It is also important to note that double string bends are much easier to control when you have more than one finger pulling on each string. It may seem odd at first, but you'll get used to it.

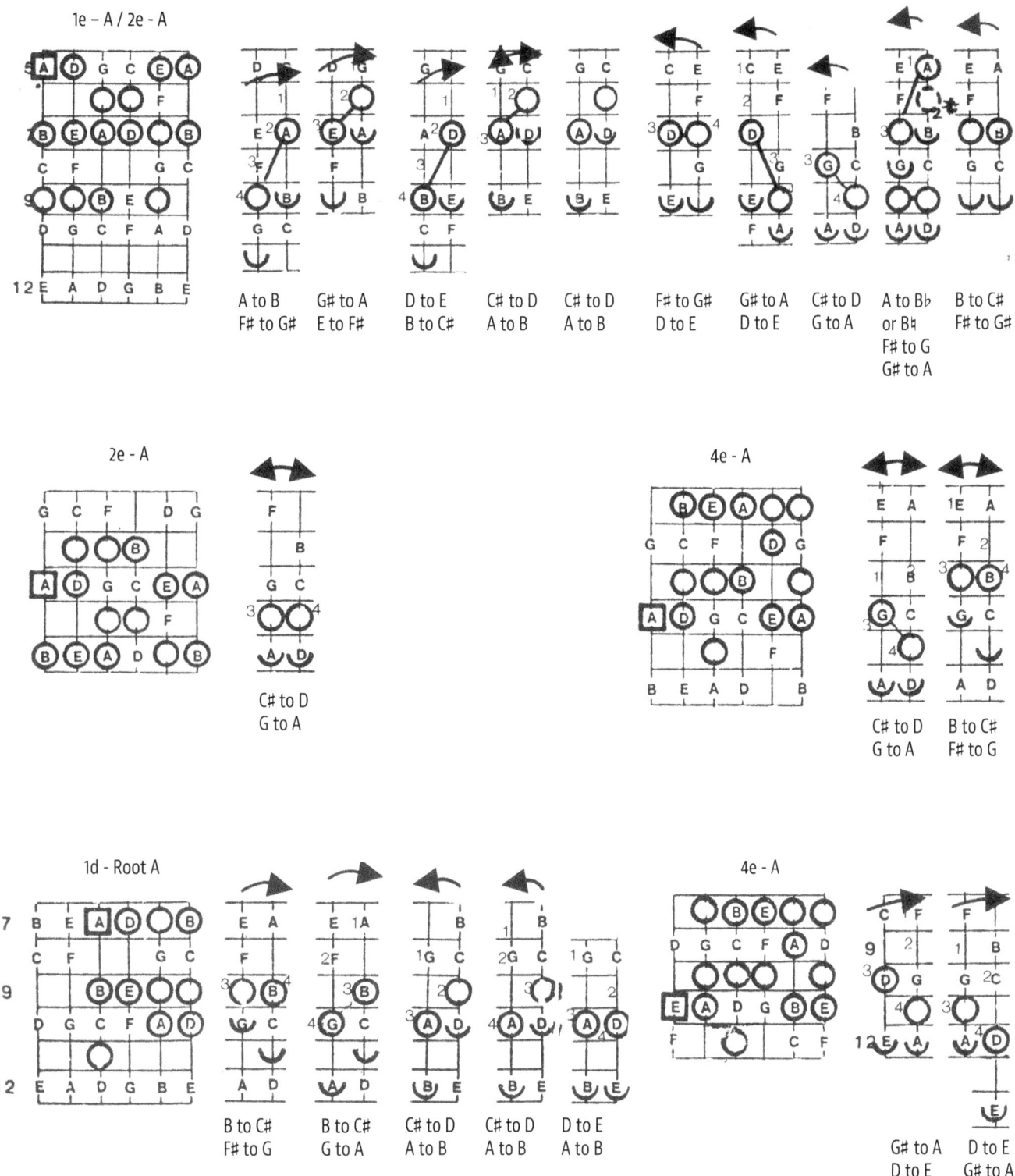

Do not become discouraged if some of these bends seem impossible at first. Check to make sure you're trying to play what's written, and then proceed slowly and carefully - listening to each string alone. If strength is all you're lacking, time and practice will solve that. Also remember that the gauge of string you use can help or hurt. If your strings are too light, you'll have to push them much farther than heavier strings to complete the same bend.

1a - Root E

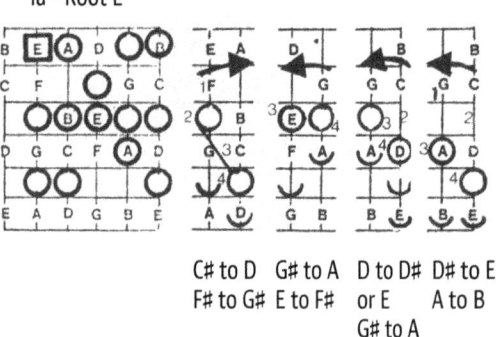

4a - Root E

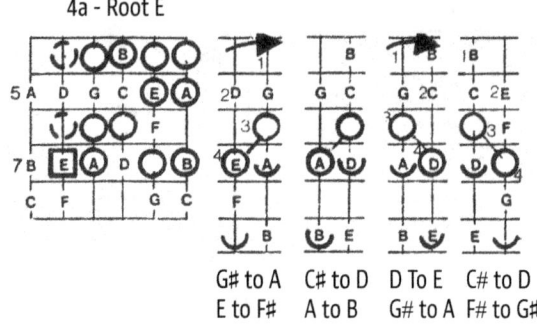

2a - Root E

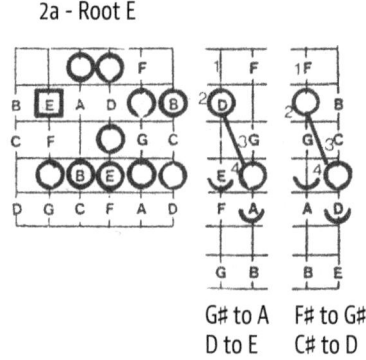

Now adjacent bends in the Key of A

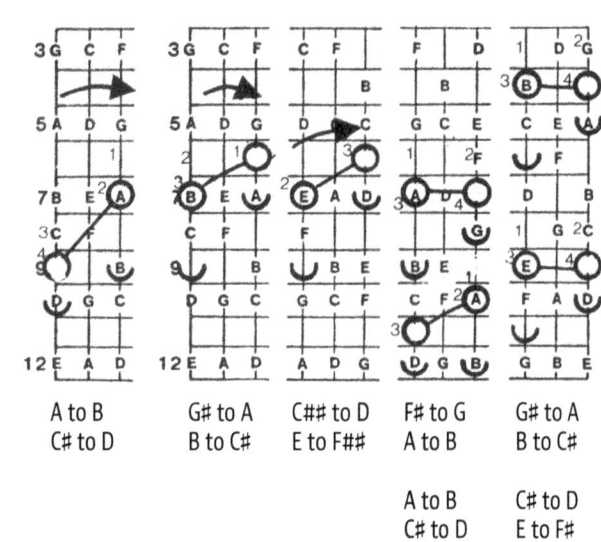

Now that you've seen some of the double bends, try relating them to the harmonized scale fingerings presented earlier. Remember - please watch your picking - make it clean, careful, and clear.

Harmony Quick Reference

The Chromatic Scale

The Notes

	C#		D#			F#		G#		A#		
C	|	D	|	E	F	|	G	|	A	|	B	C
	Db		Eb			Gb		Ab		Bb		

Scale Degrees:

Root	2	3	4	5	6	7
	9		11		13	

Major Scale Spellings and Chords

	I	ii	iii	IV	V	vi	vii	VIII	(I - Root)	Key Signatures
	Maj7	mi7	mi7	Maj7	Dom7	mi7	mi7b5	Maj7		
	C	D	E	F	G	A	B	C	C	No Accidentals
The 'Sharp' Keys	G	A	B	C	D	E	F#	G	G	1 #
	D	E	F#	G	A	B	C#	D	D	2 #
	A	B	C#	D	E	F#	G#	A	A	3 #
	E	F#	G#	A	B	C#	D#	E	E	4 #
	B	C#	D#	E	F#	G#	A#	B	B	5 #
The 'Flat' Keys	F	G	A	Bb	C	D	E	F	F	1 b
	Bb	C	D	Eb	F	G	A	Bb	Bb	2 b
	Eb	F	G	Ab	Bb	C	D	Eb	Eb	3 b
	Ab	Bb	C	Db	Eb	F	G	Ab	Ab	4 b
	Db	Eb	F	Gb	Ab	Bb	C	Db	Db	5 b
The SAME Keys	Gb	Ab	Bb	Cb	Db	Eb	F	Gb	Gb	6 b
	F#	G#	A#	B	C#	D#	E#	F#	F#	6 #
A Really Ugly Key	Cb	Db	Eb	Fb	Gb	Ab	Bb	Cb	Cb	7 b

Using the Table

The major scales are spelled from left to right. The Roman numerals are the degrees of the scale. Under each degree is the type of diatonic seventh chord found on that degree. To answer "What is the iii chord of D major?" look on the left to root D. Look across to the third degree (F#) and look up to see the chord type - minor seventh.

Key signatures are on the left with the number of accidentals used. "Which key is two sharps?" The answer is D major (or possibly B minor, but that is outside our discussion here. Sorry. B is the vi chord of D major.)

Spelling Triads and Seventh Chords

Below are shown the basic triad spellings as well as the major, minor, and dominant seventh chord spellings.

	MAJOR				Minor				Dominant 7th			
	Triad			7th	Triad			7th	Triad (major)			7th
C	C	E	G	B	C	Eb	G	Bb	C	E	G	Bb
F	F	A	C	E	F	Ab	C	Eb	F	A	C	Eb
G	G	B	D	F.	G	Bb	D	F	G	B	D	F
D	D	F#	A	C#	D	F	A	C	D	F#	A	C
A	A	C#	E	G#	A	C	E	G	A	C#	E	G
E	E	G#	B	D#	E	G	B	D	E	G#	B	D
B	B	D#	F#	A#	B	D	F#	A	B	D#	F#	A
Bb	Bb	D	F	A	Bb	Db	F	Ab	Bb	D	F	Ab
Eb	Eb	G	Bb	D	Eb	Gb	Bb	Db	Eb	G	Bb	Db
Ab	Ab	C	Eb	G	Ab	Cb	Eb	Gb	Ab	C	Eb	Gb
Db	Db	F	Ab	C	Db	Fb	Ab	Cb	Db	F	Ab	Cb
F#	F#	A#	C#	E#	F#	A	C	E	F#	A.#	C#	E
Gb	Gb	Bb	Db	F	Gb	Bbb	Db	Fb	Gb	Bb	Db	Fb

To use the table look at the examples below.

C major triad is spelled C E G.

A C major seventh chord is spelled C E G B.

A C minor seventh triad is spelled C Eb G.

A C minor seventh chord is spelled C Eb G Bb.

A C dominant seventh is composed of a C major Triad (C E G) and Bb.

A G minor seventh chord is spelled G Bb D F.

A B major seventh chord is spelled B D# F# A#.

Interval Names

Diatonic Intervals	Non-Diatonic Intervals	Enharmonic Equivalents of Non-Diatonic Intervals
C-C Unison or Prime	C-D♭ Minor 2nd	C-C♯ Augmented Prime
C-D Major 2nd	C-E♭ Minor 3rd	C-D♯ Augmented 2nd
C-E Major 3rd	C-F♭ Diminshed 4th	C-E♯ Augmented 3rd
C-F *Perfect 4th	C-G♭ Diminished 5th	C-F♯ Augmented 4th
C-G *Perfect 5th	C-A♭ Minor 6th	C-G♯ Augmented 5th
C-A Major 6th	C-B♭♭ (A) Diminished 7th C-B♭ Minor 7th	C-A♯ Augmented 6th
C-B Major 7th	C-C♭ Diminished Octave	
C up to C Octave or 'Perfect Octave'		C-B♯ Augmented 7th

The rules for naming intervals:

1. If any MAJOR interval is made SMALLER by one half step, the new resulting interval shall be called "minor." C to E is major third. C to E♭ is minor third.

2. If any PERFECT interval is made SMALLER by one half step, the new resulting interval shall be known as "DIMINISHED." C to G is a Perfect fifth. C to G♭ is a diminished fifth.

3. If any MINOR interval is made one half step smaller, the new resulting interval is also known as "DIMINISHED." The lone "C-B♭♭" interval in the middle of the table shows the diminished 7th - found in the C diminished 7th chord.

4. If a MAJOR, OR PERFECT interval, is made one half step LARGER, the new resulting interval is called "AUGMENTED." C to A is a major sixth. C to A♯ is an augmented sixth.

5. C to F♯ is an Augmented fourth. C to G♭ is a Diminished fifth. These two intervals sound the same. Why the two different names? (This is an old hang-up but still in existence.) The ♯ implies that you RAISED the F to F♯ (Augmented) while the ♭ implies that you LOWERED the G to G♭ (Diminished). It is still considered bad manners, and incorrect, to call C to F♯ a diminished fifth.

Epilogue

Thank you for using *Styles for the Studio* - investing the time and energy, practicing and thinking, and trying to make your own music. This new edition updated a lot of diagrams and text, but the contents of the original book are all here.

Over the years I've received hundreds of letters, emails, posts in forums, and 'Styles' has received listings on a number of "Top 25 Books for . . ." lists. That means a lot to me, and I hope you continue to get value from the book as you play. Music has always been one of the great joys of my life, (although it has fought me tooth and nail sometimes). Your questions and kind comments make it all the more pleasurable for me, and I am most grateful. If you have a question, you can reach me at SixStringLogic.com

Good luck as you continue with your music. Keep exploring and keep playing!

— *Leon White*

www.ingramcontent.com/pod-product-compliance
Lightning Source LLC
Chambersburg PA
CBHW080523110426
42742CB00017B/3216